202 PETS' PEEVES

Cats and Dogs Speak Out on Pesky Human Behavior

CAL OREY

CITADEL PRESS
Kensington Publishing Corp.
www.kensingtonbooks.com

CITADEL PRESS BOOKS are published by

Kensington Publishing Corp.
850 Third Avenue
New York, NY 10022

First printing: February 2003

10 9 8 7 6 5 4 3 2 1

Printed in the United States of America

Library of Congress Control Number: 2002113389

ISBN 0-8065-2442-1

Contents

Acknowledgments

During the 1970s, I hitchhiked across America with my black Labrador retriever, Stonefox, a stray dog I had picked up on a beach in San Diego. When I settled down in Northern California, a yellow Lab, whom I found through a breeder, joined us and quickly became my muse—the Golden Girl always with a tennis ball or Frisbee in her mouth.

Later on, while completing graduate school at San Francisco State University, I rescued Gandalf, a feisty gray-and-white mixed-breed cat, from the shelter. It was his bold meow that impressed me. It was as though he were saying, *Hey! I'm the one you want! Pick me!* And Alex, his best friend, an orange-and-white puss (whom I had found in a pet shop in my home town of San Jose, California), had a gentle touch and wild cat nature that gave me fifteen years of unforgettable joy.

I thank these four animal companions, who helped inspire me to write this book. Plus, I will never forget my father, a devout animal lover. He taught me to love and respect both dogs and cats—fascinating creatures who continue to make my world complete.

Foreword

In the last two decades I have visited literally hundreds of dog and cat homes where the critters were behaving badly. Their unfortunate, quirky emotional behaviors drove their humans crazy, and no matter what the owners did, the problems persisted. Some pet guardians recited the "if onlys": "If only my dog [or cat] would listen to reason," "If only my dog [or cat] would pay attention to what I tell him," "If only my dog [or cat] weren't so behaviorally challenged." Other clients were convinced good behavior was all in the showing-how: "Now, Satina, watch how Mommy climbs in the nice box, turns around, and scratches the litter! Gooood litter box," expecting the pet to take heed. The next day, the animal repeats the misdeed, and so does the owner—this time speaking louder. Do cats mind humans walking in their litter boxes?

The assumption is, of course, that there is something terribly wrong with these animals. They're already profusely pampered (just the way we like it), and this is how they return our love? When we communicate our displeasure, they stare back with a blank look. Huh? We think they're mad at us—"getting us back" for some unforgivable annoyance.

As we all know, our companion cats and dogs are more efficient at training us than we are at training them. At the dinner bowl one turned-up nose and offended look in our direction can be enough to shame us into rushing to the nearest store to buy something more attractive and palatable. (*How could I have been so callous?*) And if you're like most pet lovers, you'll agree that we're always making compromises, or even deals, to keep our pet happy. The rule seems to be something like "I'll cater to your every need if you don't chew another hole in the couch." Why don't they do as we'd like them to? What is their problem?

These critters have kept me far too busy weaving creative solutions to their quirky behaviors for me to consider it might be their humans' quirky behavior that drives them crazy. What would they tell their pet therapist if they had one?

Enter Cal Orey. At last there is a place for all of us humans to go to find out what it is that drives our pets crazy! In *202 Pets' Peeves*, Cal Orey reveals dogs' and cats' inner thoughts on the acute and chronic anthropocentric irritations they put up with from day to day. And she provides solutions to those pets' peeves in the pages that follow. Read on . . . for a fascinating look at dogs' and cats' perceptions of pesky human behaviors.

John C. Wright, Ph.D.

Certified Applied Animal Behaviorist and Author of *Ain't Misbehavin': The Groundbreaking Program for Happy, Well-Behaved Pets and Their People* (Rodale, 2001)

Preface

One evening at my cabin home in the California Sierras, my cat and dog, Kerouac and Dylan, were cuddled up with me on the sofa.

Between my two furry four-legged companions I felt very warm and very inspired. Cats and dogs, like people, I pondered, can become irked when subjected to day-to-day annoyances—pet peeves.

I recalled that earlier in the day my neighbor had paid me a visit. She had begun to give attention to my new cat, Kerouac. "He's so cute!" she had cooed, only to witness Kerouac hiss and flee.

That incident, which had included unwanted baby talk and a stranger, spawned my idea to write a problem-solution article about what irks felines. The story was titled "Your Cat's Seven Pet Peeves" and it was published by PetPlace.com, a popular pet lovers' website. Months later America Online (AOL) picked up my article on cats' pet peeves. In fact, I was later told by a PetPlace.com editor that it had received more than eight hundred thousand hits in one year!

Meanwhile, I continued writing about pets, as I shared my life with my cat and dog. I soon realized that my beloved animal companion pair had a lot more than seven peeves on their minds.

As a single and isolated author and journalist living in a quiet paradise, who has written about cats and dogs for fifteen years, I couldn't help but take serious note of my cat's and dog's day-to-day pet peeves. I tuned in to the town's stray dogs and feral cats, and the neighborhood cats and dogs, too. Also, I remembered what had irked my past companion animals.

Then it hit me! *What if I wrote a book about disgruntled cats and dogs everywhere?* It seemed appropriate to have my two best friends, Kerouac and Dylan, be the spokespets for cats and dogs. I quickly decided to let my favorite cat and dog voice their common pet complaints and gripes (as told to me).

The ultimate goal of my book *202 Pets' Peeves: Cats and Dogs Speak Out on Pesky Human Behavior* is to share my journalistic insight and pet awareness with cat and dog lovers. I aim to educate and amuse pet people on how pesky human behavior can drive cats and dogs crazy. With the guidance of my two fur children and animal experts I explain how it's time to listen up. As a result, you will discover that it is never too late to learn new human tricks. Then you can begin to cut down your cat's or dog's pets' peeve list to a more acceptable size.

The Peeves of Pets

Is your cat or dog a bundle of nerves? Does Fluffy or Fido complain by hissing, howling, or heading for the hills? Would you like a way to find out what gets your cat's or dog's goat? If the answer to any one of these questions is yes, then you need this book! I'm a self-proclaimed pet expert and lover. I am a writer who works at home in the presence of my cat and dog. As usual, my cat is on my lap, and my dog is at my feet. What they have in common are pet peeves.

Like me, countless other people, perhaps even you, have experienced the fallout pet peeves can have on a cat's or dog's body, mind, and spirit. But we're often clueless as to why certain things have such a big impact on their health and well-being. All we know is that they do.

To introduce you to the pets' point of view, I've chosen Kerouac, a two-and-a-half-year-old mixed-breed cat, and Dylan, a twelve-and-a-half-year-old sporting dog breed, to be the spokespets for *202 Pets' Peeves: Cats and Dogs Speak Out on Pesky Human Behavior.* Kerouac is a sassy and hip black-and-white all-American domestic longhaired feline, and Dylan is a sensitive and wise orange-and-white Brittany—the typical pets next door. Without inhibitions, they speak out on pet peeves and pesky human behavior.

Wrong cat food? An anti-cat mate? Anti-dog lodging? Dog ageist attitude? You'll experience vicariously what irks four-leggers and what you can do about it. Divided into two parts, *202 Pets' Peeves* will describe your feline's 101 pet peeves and your canine's 101 pet peeves. Furthermore, the two parts will each be divided into body, mind, and spirit peeves. And some peeves will tickle the funny bones of people who love both cats and dogs.

My literary cat, Kerouac, and fun-loving dog, Dylan, will define what each pet peeve is, voice their catty complaints and doggone gripes, provide solutions, and offer tips (from pet surveys to pet-friendly services). Also, some pet peeves will be addressed in greater depth to provide humans with a better understanding of the nuisances.

With backup from animal experts, Kerouac and Dylan will provide personal anecdotes and cutting-edge information for pet lovers looking for ways to add happiness (and years) to their pet's life. Most importantly, once you discover what gets your pet's goat—and fix it—your proactive actions will help you to enhance the human–animal bond, which can make your tail wag, too.

PART ONE

Your Feline's
101 Pet Peeves

(From the Cat's
Perspective)

1. Body Hisses

Pet Peeve #1
Food With Killer Chemicals

I admit it. I'm finicky. I'll turn my nose at the scent of the wrong cat food. But some humans just don't get it. There's to-die-for healthful cat foods on the market. Still, in the cupboards of American homes sits a bag (or two) of cat food labeled with a cat's tail list of deadly ingredients.

Did you know that many commercial brands of pet food are lacking in the vitamins, minerals, and fiber needed to support a cat's health? Truth is, it's hard to know what you're buying. Unfortunately, many commercial brands of pet food are made from food by-products considered unfit for human consumption. Translation: They're unfit for us as well. ("Hiss!") For example, propyl gallate, which is added to retard spoilage, is suspected of causing liver damage. Butylated hydroxytoluene (BHT), another morsel found in commercial pet food, may cause fetal abnormalities. Oh my kittens!

Purr-fect Solution If you won't play Super Chef (I bet they cook for their furry friends), may I suggest that you buy all-natural cat foods? These shouldn't contain fillers, sugar, chemical preservatives, artificial colorings, or synthetic flavorings.

If you buy my fave natural quality brand in quantity, you'll save money and I will feel secure.

Feline Tip Whatever you decide to buy, use your cat's eye to find a statement on the product label claiming that the food has met the Association of American Feed Control Officials (AAFCO) procedures to provide complete and balanced nutrition for my age.

Pet Peeve #2
No-Name Chow

While throwing out the killer cat food, dump the No-Name cat kibble, too. Cat food that comes in a generic bag is bad news. Not only are you being cheap, it tastes yucky. Even the dog won't eat it! Why should I? Holistic vets (docs who treat pets with natural therapies) insist that the key to disease prevention is not found in the typical commercial pet foods. So do you really think good nutrition is going to be found in a low-cost bag of bland No-Name? Get real.

Purr-fect Solution Cats are a Class Act. We love designer labels for cats. It makes us feel good—an ego-boost. Natural commercial premium foods with a household-word brand name contain all-human-grade ingredients and are preserved with disease-fighting antioxidant vitamins. These can include vitamin C, which helps boost the immune system and staves off disease, and heart-healthy E, which improves circulation by helping the heart beat better. That means you may improve my cat life by using premium brands of cat chow.

Pet Peeve #3
Meatless Meals

Let's be honest: Cats are carnivores with a capital C. Read: We need our meat. Yet you cook up a batch of lean chuck or hamburger for yourself (or the begging dog) and ignore my natural meat cravings! Why do you do that? Cats require high levels of protein compared to dogs, as well as taurine, an amino acid found in many meats.

Purr-fect Solution   Raw meat contains plenty of taurine, so feed us raw or lightly cooked meat or poultry once in a while. Some good choices are beef, chicken, turkey, and lamb. And note, save the rabbit food for the dog. We felines are not vegetarians (although a small amount of grains and veggies is good for us). FYI: Taurine is found in cat supplements, too.

Feline Tip   To find a holistic vet in your area and obtain a cat food recipe (with meat) custom-tailored for your cat, contact the American Holistic Veterinary Medical Association. Log on to www.ahvma.org, or call (410) 569-0795. Speaking of meat . . .

Pet Peeve #4
No Home Cookin'

Why don't you ever whip us up a tasty home-cooked cat meal (including lean meat)? Being an independent cat, I can understand that standing over a hot stovetop may not fit into your self-serving cat-like lifestyle. It bugs me, however, when you get bit by the home-maker bug and prepare a meat-based dish but exclude me. How can you cook and eat a juicy hamburger or liver giblets in front of me—the carnivorous cat! It's pathetic that I am left out of this cookfest.

Purr-fect Solution Next time you get an itch to hit the kitchen, give me kibble combined with raw meat and veggies. You can either make it yourself (once you get the recipe) or use a prepared home-style cat food.

Feline Tip For more information about home-style cat food (which contains real meat, grains, and vegetables), contact a holistic vet for a custom-tailored recipe. (Refer to Pet Peeve #3.)

Pet Peeve #5
Overfeeding Me

If you're dishing up the No-Name stuff (or giving me fatty snacks), one day I may resemble that lasagna-eating orange Garfield, the pudgy cartoon cat. But letting me pig out is no laughing matter! What irks me is I then hear your friends say, "Has Kitty put on a few extra pounds?" How insensitive! It's not our fault if we are fighting the battle of the bulge. Humans are in charge of a cat's diet, right? Worse, if you don't keep me lean and fit, excess fat may make my heart work harder, make me diabetes-prone, and shorten my mouse-chasing days.

Purr-fect Solution To melt my fat away, go back to Pet Peeve #4 and consider preparing me home-cooked cat food. My best bet? An all-natural, raw-meat diet that includes organic protein, whole grains, raw veggies, and healthy oils. Because it's rich in vitamins, minerals, fiber, and living enzymes (good for my digestion), it'll support my health—and preserve my lean-and-mean kittenlike body.

Pet Peeve #6
No Water Refills

If I can't find fresh food in my cat bowl, how can I expect to get fresh water, essential to a pet's diet? Don't yell at me if I have to dip my furry cat paw into your glass of calorie-free Calistoga with a lemon twist. It bugs me that you sip on the good bottled stuff while I must fend for myself. Ever wonder why I hang out at the water faucet in the kitchen or bathroom? Surprise! Cats, like humans, need their H_2O fix for good health and well-being. (I hit the fish tank for the adrenaline rush.) But the tap water that you give us may be polluted with toxic chemicals such as lead and arsenic. So while you're enjoying that fresh springwater, think of poor Kitty lapping up the bad stuff.

Purr-fect Solution Don't despair. Just let me get what you get: fresh water (bottled or distilled). That way I can feel better from head to paws (just like you), because it flushes those killer toxins from my body. If you're mumbling, "I can't afford to keep my cat in bottled water," may I suggest that we invest in a water purifier or buy bottled water in bulk?

Feline Tip Consider ordering one of those continuously running water products for self-reliant, health-conscious cats. That way we can get fresh water whether you're around or not.

Pet Peeve #7
Being Anti–Pet Supplements

Every morning you take your vitamins with a glass of fresh water. You wouldn't think of missing your daily supplement. But what about me—your cat? It annoys me that you supplement your diet with essential vitamins and minerals but you don't think that I may need added food supplements. By being anti–pet supplements, it makes me feel like you're leaving my good health and feline longevity in Lady Luck's hands. ("Hiss!")

Purr-fect Solution Holistic vets suggest that I, like humans, take those disease-fighting supplements, vitamins C and E. Also, check out vitamin formulas that are targeted for certain age groups, which may help us stay on mouse patrol in our golden years.

Pet Peeve #8
Dogged Treats

Taking your daily vitamins and excluding me from your healthful regimen is one thing, but giving me the dog's treats or not giving me any yummies at all is unacceptable human behavior. You give the dog treats. I've seen you do it. "Here, Dylan. Mommy wants to give you a doggy treat." But what about me? Hello. Cats have cravings, too. And it just so happens that cat treats is one of them.

Purr-fect Solution Healthful kitty snacks are what I should be getting—despite my desperate urge to eat the human or dog stuff. Some good choices? Personally, I love low-fat, high-protein water-packed albacore tuna. (I know it's pricey, but it's heart-healthy fish.) Plus, dipping my furry paw into your low-fat yogurt is a thrill, too.

Feline Tip For special cat treats, log on to the Internet and check out pet companies.

Pet Peeve #9
Human Junk Food

It's one thing to stock the cupboards with doggy delights and no cat treats, but trying to off your junk food on me is disgusting! Please don't underestimate my feline intelligence. I'm not a Junk-Food Junkie! So why do people off their potato chips, fast food, lunch meat, and candy on me—the cat? FYI: A bag of chewy gummy bears will not tempt us to perform canine tricks. I'm a finicky and traditional cat. Read: I prefer hamburger and turkey.

Purr-fect Solution As you know, I'm trying to keep fit and lean, so instead of junk food I'd rather have commercial-brand specialty cat foods any day. Cat foods such as those labeled "light" to help pare pounds are certainly better than human fast food chock-full of fat and empty calories. Save the fast-food fixes for the dog.

Pet Peeve #10
Litter Box Neglect

Why do you have a catfit when I use the houseplants for my litter box? If the cat litter has a pungent odor to the point that I must find a clothespin to clip on my nose, it's my option, as a self-reliant cat, to take my business to cleaner quarters. A stinky cat box is not one of my favorite things. I'm not about to get my paws dirty. The fact is, we are obsessive-compulsive critters, and if the litter is not scent-sational we'll go elsewhere.

Purr-fect Solution A rule of paw: When the litter box smells bad to you, it reads *Danger: Off Limits!* to me, the sensitive cat with amazing olfactory powers. (We can smell things humans can't.) Jot this down: Clean the litter box at least every other day and stick to it. Just do it. And I promise to keep out of your potted plants.

Pet Peeve #11
No Privacy

Imagine: The bathroom is clean, nobody is around, and it's time to go. I assume the position—and in walks the dog or a human! You'd hate it, too. But I have to deal with lack of privacy every day. It seems that when the litter box is good to go (or the room that it's in is vacant), I am the last one to know it. Worse, after I finish up the dog sniffs around for tasty tidbits. ("Hissss.") What's a cat to do?

Purr-fect Solution May I suggest looking into one of those hooded-type litter boxes? Instead of the traditional open litter box, one with a hood like an igloo is inviting. No one can see me do my cat thing day or night. No matter if my cat box is in the bathroom or laundry room, I will have ultimate privacy without any intruders. These state-of-the-art litter boxes are available at pet stores.

Pet Peeve #12
Not Ranking Litters

These days there are so many cat litters to choose from that it can confuse a human and a cat. It irks me when my human changes litters because we cats don't like change. As animal experts say, "If it ain't broke, don't fix it." We cats agree.

Purr-fect Solution Even though *change* isn't in my vocabulary I began to wonder if other kinds of litter may have better odor control or less tracking so my human isn't always cleaning up after me. (That's embarrassing.) So I did my homework. Check out my test results in the table below.

LITTER RANKINGS

Litter Type	Ingredients	Odor Control	Tracking	Rating
Regular Clay	Clay	Good	Moderate; it works for me	4 Paws Up
Fine-grain clumping	Clay, cedar flakes, deodorizer	Excellent	It's like a sandy beach	1½ Paws Up
Wood pellets	Woods: pine, aspen, etc.	Smells fresh	Hmmm; not my fantasy	2 Paws Up
Plant by-products	Granulated wheat, grain, pellets of grass, etc.	No smell	Little	3 Paws Up
Paper by-products	Pellets from recycled paper	Odor-free	Little	3 Paws Up
Silica gel	Round particles of silica gel	No smell	Beads everywhere	1 Paw Up

After my test run of the six basic types of litter (there are many brands available for each), I've decided that regular clay (unscented) is my fave. But note, each cat is different and has different litter preferences. In other words, while my personal choice of litter makes my day, it may ruin the next cat's.

Pet Peeve #13
Dog Leash Walking

Ever see a happy cat on a leash or in a harness? Perhaps three out of one hundred felines can do the dog leash walk thing—but you can count me out. This peeve is not an easy one to solve. Yes, I love the great outdoors. But no, I detest being held back by an uptight human who has me on a short leash. It's an insult to my wild cat ancestors. I'd rather commune with nature without having to take a human along with me. What a drag!

Purr-fect Solution It's cool that cat people home in to our natural instincts to want to get back to nature. After all, it isn't safe roaming the neighborhood these days. Dogs, cars, and cat gangs can spook indoor cats like me. I guess it wouldn't hurt to lighten up and consider going for a stroll on a cat leash. (Can I wear sunglasses so my cat friends won't recognize me?)

Feline Tip For more information about cat leashes and harnesses, go to pet stores such as PETsMART and Petco.

Pet Peeve #14
Boring Cat-Aerobics

Unlike dogs, I don't do exercise. Repeat: Cats don't do exercise. But if I do get the urge to get a move on, it will be on my terms. I abhor b-o-r-i-n-g pet workouts. Jogging and the doggy treadmill aren't going to do the trick. Sorry. I just don't see me sweating like a dog— at least not in this century.

Purr-fect Solution I do know that creative cat play can help keep me heart-healthy, improve my muscle tone, and burn fat and calories. I suggest we team up and play with interactive cat toys such as Cat Teasers. You can place the teaser in one hand, wave a colored feathered cat toy from left to right, and watch me happily chase the toy until I pounce on it. Repeat for effect (my enjoyment).

Feline Tip Check out website pet stores, Petco, and PETsMART for other available interactive cat toys, such as Fly Toys.

Pet Peeve #15
No Time for Play

Once I start a cat-aerobicize program, you might slack off (or allow me to). Or just when I think things have changed with our new-and-improved fun time, you disappear. ("Yeroowwll.") It irks me when you would rather read the newspaper than watch my latest kitty rollover trick on the front page. Or when you're sleeping and I want to play Blanket Monster, and you shoo me away. Hey, what happened to your sense of fun and spontaneity?

Purr-fect Solution Watch me play in a paper bag or cardboard box and seize the cat moment. Go ahead—join me. If you can't find time for me, one day when I am gone you will say, "I wish I had played with Kitty more" or "He was such a playful puss." (Just kidding.) Lighten up!

Pet Peeve #16
Bad Hairball Days

Ack! Ack! Hairballs happen when my fur (which I lick and consume) collects in my tummy. Just thinking about hairballs irritates me. Not only is it disturbing for me to cough up a hairball, but it's worse when I hear those three human words, "No! Not there!" Sometimes, I don't have control over where the brown mass, often gummy-worm-shaped, comes up. It just does.

Purr-fect Solution First and foremost, don't be catty. It's not our fault. If you brush us regularly (especially longhaired cats like me) and add some fiber to our diet (such as oat bran), it may do the trick and keep me hairball-free. It may also save you cleaning fees for that Oriental rug or pricey leather sofa. But if I'm still plagued by annoying hairballs, let's go to the vet and find out if I have any food allergies.

Feline Tip There are hairball remedy products and anti-hairball cat foods available at pet stores.

Pet Peeve #17
Irregular Checkups

How do you think we feel when you check out yourself (or the dog) on a daily basis while we independent cats sit pretty and ignored next to a hairball? (Remember me, Kerouac? I have long black hair.) It's so unfair! Cats like regular routine checkups just like humans. Aren't cats included in the equal rights amendment?

Purr-fect Solution   We deserve human hands-on treatment every day. By looking for parasites and signs of illness, you can help us detect feline woes early and prevent a major cat crisis. Yearly vet visits and biannual checkups for senior cats can help detect and ward off disease. I don't want to be pushy, but I am your fur child. Contact your local humane society and/or pet store and find out the dates they offer discount pet vaccinations.

Feline Tip   Subscribe to the monthly *Catnip* newsletter by Belvoir Publishing and keep up to date on cat health care. To order twelve issues for $24, call (800) 829-0926.

Pet Peeve #18
No Medical Benefits

In case you get sick, you've got a medical plan, right? But what about me—the cat? I don't like to complain, but I'm not *that* independent! What if I get ill or need medical attention? Can you afford to take care of me? When I curl up next to you at night I lie awake worrying, *What if I get a strange and deadly kitty illness that requires big bucks?* Is that any way for a cat to live? Cat people should write a letter to the White House about getting a national cat medical package plan.

Purr-fect Solution Pet insurance can help take care of me in case I get sick or get in an accident. Cats will be cats. Whoops! (Remember when I got stuck behind the refrigerator?) Pet insurance offers coverage for accidents and illnesses, provides routine care coverage to help pay for an annual vet exam, shots—and more.

Feline Tip For more information, call companies such as Veterinary Pet Insurance at (800) 872-7387 or log on to petinsurance.com to see what it's all about.

Pet Peeve #19
Lousy Dental Plan

Humans have medical insurance and go to the dentist twice a year. But what about me—the cat? I have teeth, too. It bugs me that humans think cats are totally self-reliant—like we can brush our own teeth? Worse, why don't you tend to my pearly whites like you do your own? Equally important to annual dental exams is home dental care, which means brushing my teeth at least three times per week.

Purr-fect Solution The American Animal Hospital Association (AAHA) recommends the following for both younger and older cats, although it's easier to start when we are young:

- To introduce me to brushing, wrap gauze or a washcloth around your finger and use it like a toothbrush. Wipe all my teeth, front and back, with strokes from the gum line to the tip of the tooth. Do this for one to two weeks until I'm familiar with having my gums and teeth rubbed.

- Gradually progress to a soft toothbrush and water. After a week of using a soft toothbrush, add a small amount of special cat toothpaste. Never use human toothpaste because it can irritate our stomach. Forget using a human toothbrush. We now have dental products, from toothbrushes to toothpaste, available to us.

- Begin by brushing the front teeth and then move to the back. The bristles should be held at a 45-degree angle to the tooth surface and moved in an oval motion. Scrub the crevice where the gums meet the teeth, because this is where odor and infection begin.

Pet Peeve #20
Hiding the Herbs

I've noticed that when humans get sick or stressed out, they'll use herbal remedies. But what about us? Have you ever thought that herbs, derived from Mother Nature, may help cats get through rocky times, too? It gets my goat that you'll turn your nose up at cat herbal remedies when that's maybe all it'll take to make me feel better. If herbs work for you, why not for me? I thought we had an equal relationship.

Purr-fect Solution By using herbs when I have a health problem, you can boost my well-being. Not only can Chinese herbs such as ginseng help enhance my immunity, but they can also lessen my stress. Other good herbs to use are dandelion and burdock, which may help me recover faster from a chronic disease.

Feline Tip To find out more about herbs for cats, check out your local health food store's pet section. For the recommended dosage, consult your vet.

Pet Peeve #21
Anti–Alternative Cat Care

Other natural remedies can keep me healthy in the twenty-first century, too. But you need to know what's out there. I know that you have been bringing home human natural alternatives (such as aromatherapy candles and essential oils). Like you, I'm not totally against mainstream medicine, but I prefer going back to the basics. I'd rather keep healthy from head to tail than wait until medications or surgery are required.

Purr-fect Solution Don't be surprised that we are climbing onto the alternative care bandwagon. "Most of today's practitioners use alternative medicines allopathically—confronting disease directly," says Randy Kidd, D.V.M., of McLouth, Kansas. "Practitioners will ultimately have to learn to use the alternative medicines in their natural manner—relying on the patient's innate body, mind, and spirit itself to return to a state of health."

As a result, we cats know that the use of alternative pet care (for example, herbal remedies and massage) will help us stay happy and healthy. Cat massage, for instance, will help relax me. Rub me (gently please) from head to tail. It wouldn't hurt to look for suspicious lumps or pesky parasites while you're at it. Plus, cat massage is free. Go to the website www.catmassage.com and learn more about it. To order the Cat Massage Video, call (877) MEOW-MEOW.

Feline Tip For more information, contact AltVetMed (alternative veterinary medicine) at www.altvetmed.com.

Pet Peeve #22
Dogged Baths

Why do humans think that feline gods of cleanliness need a bath, any-how? Imagine that you are a cat. You're feeling warm and fuzzy as you sun yourself in a windowsill. Suddenly a human picks you up and dumps you into a cold sink. Then, water, soap, and plenty of wrestling takes place. Hmmm. The scenario reminds me of the anti-water witch in *The Wizard of Oz* who when wet screams: "I'm melting!"

Purr-fect Solution To get cats to tolerate a bath, you can begin with the "behavioral procedure called shaping," says Mary Burch, Ph.D., a certified animal behaviorist in Tallahassee, Florida. Shaping is where you take baby steps to teach a new skill. Here are Dr. Burch's anti-dogged-cat-bath pointers [please note my feline-related editorial notes]:

- Begin by putting Kitty in a few inches of warm water for a short time. [Help! I'm melting. Just kidding.]

- Take Kitty out of the water and immediately praise and offer a treat just before drying. [Like we're going to have an appetite?]

- In each successive bathing experience, add a little more water and gradually add shampooing until you are able to bathe Kitty's whole body. [This may take years.]

If cat bathing sounds too painful to you, taking me to a kitty spa can make my life (and yours) a lot easier. Or, consider mobile grooming so we aren't bothered by cages or barking dogs, and you don't get wet or scratched.

Feline Tip Check out the Yellow Pages for mobile pet groomers in your area. It may cost you more than taking me to a pet groomer, but I'm worth it.

Pet Peeve #23
Declawing

Speaking of scratching . . . Declawing cats is absurd. Whoever thought of removing our claws should be sent to Jupiter (without cats!). My ten claws are my defense against bully dogs, catty cats, and other fear factors in the world. If you declaw me, what am I supposed to do to remain a self-reliant cat? It hurts me to even think about such an inhumane procedure.

Purr-fect Solution Humans often will think of declawing us when we shred their prized possessions, right? To save your costly furniture, a transparent, acrylic-based, nontoxic product won't hurt me or your pocketbook. Or you can check out cat scratch posts to help keep me from clawing your fave stuff. Also, some cats wear those Soft Paws nail caps, which may help you cope with our scratching fetish.

Pet Peeve #24
Flea Unawareness

If you declaw me, how will I scratch my fleas? Those bloodsuckers love to jump for joy on warm-blooded cats, like me. It bugs me that you act clueless when I've definitely got a flea in my ear. Fleas are annoying little pests. It's not fair that I have to be on flea patrol 24/7. Worse, if you spray me with toxic flea killers, I'm hitting the highway. (It's safer.)

Purr-fect Solution I prefer to stay flea-free naturally. Flea repellents like brewer's yeast and garlic have micronutrients and odors that stop fleas in their tracks naturally. Also, herb-based, non-toxic flea (and tick) shampoos include natural ingredients. Other inexpensive methods? Try vacuuming the carpet frequently and combing my hair with a flea comb to keep me flea-free. Yes, we are worth the trouble.

Pet Peeve #25
Unsafe Cat Collars

Now that I'm flea-free (or you're working on it), what's with the anti-flea cat collar? It's full of toxins. If my collar is unnatural or not comfy (read: too tight or too loose), it's another risk to my health and happiness. Worse, if I don't have proper identification tags, it will make my life miserable if I ever run away and can't find my way back home. I don't have time to worry about these things. That's your job.

Purr-fect Solution The rule of paw is, if you can fit a human index finger under my collar, it's okay. But if you can't, call 9-1-1 now. ("Meow.") Just kidding. But hey, keep tabs on the fit of my cat collar. Also, do you know that some cat collars come with latches that snap open in case I should happen to get caught on an object during my feline leaps and bounds? Cool, huh?

Pet Peeve #26
High-Rise Windows

I like to sit on the windowsill and watch the butterflies and birds outside. Often I will even jump at a passing bird, bumping into a window—or falling out of an open window. If I do fall out of a window (especially in a high-rise building), I can fall victim to high-rise syndrome—and you'll find your beloved puss featured in a story on the eleven o'clock news. While we do have an efficient righting mechanism (a falling cat will orient himself so that he will hit in a diver's position—front feet first, and then nose), it's not perfect.

Purr-fect Solution The best way to prevent a high-rise-dwelling cat from falling is to be aware that it can happen. In addition:

- Install tightly secured screens in windows that do not have screens.

- For apartment dwellers who rarely open a window, except when strange humans such as maintenance people visit, put me in a safe room that will not be entered or exited.

- To prevent your getting a hospital bill that can hit $2,000 and my getting a kitty body cast, consider investing in strong and secure cat-friendly windows, which will cost much less.

Feline Tip Kitty sills (heated ones, too) that bring the outdoors to me are available at pet stores.

Pet Peeve #27
Pricey Furniture

Got a leather couch? Stereo speakers? I can't help myself. If I'm having a bad hairball day, bored, or hungry, like other cats I have to scratch something. It's a cat thing. Oriental rugs? Silk sheets? Hate 'em. They drive domestic cats wild. It's the traction! I have to dig my claws into the stuff. I detest my human's jiggly waterbed, too. (Darn hippie!) Those water bubbles are irresistible. The catch is, a human's "bad cat!" words will interrupt but won't stop my attack on the pricey stuff.

Purr-fect Solution You've got three options, O materialistic one: First, we can go back to orange crates and plastic dorm-room cubes (and play like we're starving college students). Second, you can tape or tack on heavy vinyl or other smooth material over the arms and back of your pricey sofa. Or third, we can go cat furniture shopping till we drop.

Pet Peeve #28
Dirt, Dust, and Chemicals

Speaking of furniture, cats are neatniks. A few days ago, while waiting for my human to come home, I began nibbling on her potted houseplants. (Dirt on my paws ruined my fun.) Later, while playing Chase the Toy Mouse, dust bunnies sabotaged my catch. ("Aachoo!") But my cat's curiosity about those household cleaning products under the kitchen sink may be the demise of me yet. Even though I might try to get into them, they may make me sicker than a dog. Don't forget, we're cats, and humans are supposed to watch out for their fur children. "Aaa-choo!"

Purr-fect Solution What's a responsible cat owner to do? I've come up with some all-natural tips that will keep a house cat-friendly:

- Use natural fibers for our bedding (organic cotton and wool).

- Avoid carpets which are mold magnets and can make cats sick. Personally, I like hardwood floors.

- Ventilate the house well to reduce indoor air pollution. Don't allow smoking.

- Don't confine us to a garage, basement, or bathroom that contains household chemicals.

- Fill your home with hardy houseplants such as philodendrons to help wipe out those pollutants in your house naturally. (Warning: Hang up to keep cat-nibble-free.) Plants filter the air like vacuums and suck up airborne pollution.

Feline Tip For more information, contact organizations such as the National Animal Poison Control Center at the University of Illinois at (888) 426-4435 or (800) 548-2423.

Pet Peeve #29
Cluttered Counters

Household countertops that have clutter, from too many books to toiletries, are not cat-friendly, either. Cluttered counters wreak havoc with a cat's feline grace and balance. When I imitate Tom Cruise's dance routine in *Risky Business* (which includes skidding on the floor), it's a drag when clutter holds me back from slipping and sliding on a clean surface. It's not fun when I can't make a clean getaway without a cluttered head-on collision and pileup.

Purr-fect Solution Please declutter our life. Translation: Go for a more contemporary, simple, streamlined, cat-friendly look. Box the human magazine issues and books you don't need and give them to your local library. Recycle the old newspapers (let me shred them first). And when you open your mail, toss out the junk—but save all the cat-related stuff (such as coupons and cat magazine offers).

Pet Peeve #30
Being Stepped On

We are small creatures who often get underfoot. (The average adult cat is 6 to 8 pounds.) So when we are squashed by a big human's foot, it feels like King Kong has made his pawprint on us. ("Mmmm"—please refer to Pet Peeve #40 for a feline translation.) The harder you step, the more it hurts. We take our tails very seriously. The tail "isn't just a nice decoration—this is a communication device," explains Dr. Burch.

Purr-fect Solution According to Dr. Burch, "If you have a cat that is constantly underfoot, you would be wise to teach yourself to 'look first, then step.'" Or may I suggest that when you are passing through, you announce yourself (a loudspeaker would be nice): "Human approaching." This, in turn, will help you save the cat tails in the world.

2. Mind Games

Pet Peeve #31
Obsessive Cat Collectors

People who collect cats often do it out of the goodness of their heart. But sometimes, a few stray cats in a home end up being a hundred needy cats in a disorderly household. It is difficult to hold a real job and spoil even one self-serving cat. Imagine how hard it is to feed, groom, and tend to the medical care of dozens of us? The human odds are high that cat neglect will occur, sooner or later. Another Kerouacism.

Purr-fect Solution If you are a dedicated cat rescuer, you want to avoid feeling overwhelmed like the poor old woman (in the Mother Goose nursery rhyme) who lived in a shoe and had too many kids. Are you buying cat food and litter 24/7? Does your house smell like an unattended litter box? Did you get another vet bill with a red PAYMENT OVERDUE stamp on it? If the answer to these questions is yes, it's time to recruit some help.

Feline Tip Contact your local humane society to find out if they can help by finding foster homes for some of your kitties.

Pet Peeve #32
Anti-Cat People

What's worse than people who collect cats and are irresponsible caretakers? Ailurophobes—people who fear cats. This is not the medieval period, when respect and admiration for cats plummeted. Did you know that according to cat lore, in some parts of Asia it is believed that if you are afraid of cats, you must have been a rat in your last life? Enough said.

Purr-fect Solution Do you know people who have a cat phobia? It's time for your friends to face the fear. Suggest to the ailurophobes that they visit people who are owned by cats. In time they, too, will enjoy the many healing powers of cats. (We help humans relax, fight heart disease, boost the immune system, beat loneliness, comfort the sick and elderly, and boost longevity.) One good way to convert aulirophobes to cat lovers is to have them get involved and support animal organizations.

Feline Tip Check with humane societies such as The Humane Society of the United States about public-awareness campaigns or activist alerts. Call (202) 452-1100 or log on to www.hsus.org.

Pet Peeve #33
People Who Say Cats Are Sneaky

Anti-cat people are quick to quip that "cats are sneaky," which is annoying to cats and cat lovers. The witch-and-cat days are over—but when I hear people mumble "cats are sneaky," it makes me wonder. Centuries ago, many folks believed that witches could turn themselves into cats and that these cats would do the witches' bidding, performing good or bad deeds. I suppose this is sneaky behavior, but the images of bad witches and bad cats are fading.

Purr-fect Solution Envision the twenty-first-century "good" cat with traits that are linked to "good" sneakiness such as craftiness and slyness. In fact, you can learn a few catlike tricks from us that can help you at work and at home. Sure, we may tinkle in strange places and hide our toys where no human can find them, but we know how to keep a secret—and have our treats, too. It's not really sneaky behavior. It's being cat smart.

Pet Peeve #34
Unsupervised Infants

While cats can live in peace with babies (with much better odds than cats cohabiting with folks who tag us as sneaky), we still have a few complaints. For starters, when we feel ignored by our "parents," we may become miffed. Also, a baby's cries can upset our equilibrium. I can personally attest to this. I'm not used to constant noise. In other words, bringing home a baby, especially one who cries, can be a nuisance because it is a change, which cats, like me, don't take kindly to. You see, cats think *Before baby, I was the baby.* Then *bam!* Their human's attention is elsewhere. If the attention to me is zapped without adequate warning, I may suffer from the kitty blues.

Purr-fect Solution To prevent this from happening, before the baby is born consider adding another cat to our household. If it's a compatible match, the feline companionship will be a nice diversion for me when you forget my name. Another idea is that before the baby comes home, occasionally play a recording of a baby crying. (Go to a baby nursery and tape triplets.) This may help get me (and you) desensitized to the new sound. Earplugs for cats are another option. But overall, take heart. Cats and babies can be mixed. All it takes is preparation and catlike persistence.

Pet Peeve #35
Children Who Think Cats Are Toys

Toddlers, unlike infants, are clever little people, aren't they? But we can handle being toyed with only so much. Sure, I like to play (I'm a cat), but I am not a stuffed tiger or a wind-up critter. I am a real live feline, and grasping my tail or a hunk of my fur is not my idea of cat's play. ("Meow!") And then doting human parents wonder why Fluffy scratched Pretty Polly. Go figure.

Purr-fect Solution   If you show kids the right way to hold us (with my back legs held by one arm and my front legs held by the other), it's one paw forward. For the record, I detest being picked up by my front legs only. Think of a relative who picked you up under the arms and cooed, "You're so cute." Not fun, huh? Please teach children that I am a whimsical cat. Respect my unpredictable feline personality. This can make the beginning of a wonderful child–cat relationship.

Feline Tip   Toddler-friendly cat breeds include the Bombay, Maine coon and Scottish fold.

Pet Peeve #36
Lapless People

Kids and adults without available laps can be a problem for us when we want to hop into a safe, cozy place and curl up. If you shoo me out of your lap, it makes me think, *Excuse me.* And because I'm a persistent creature I will jump back into your lap again and again. Hey, I know that you know that I want affection and/or attention and I don't like rejection. Who does?

Purr-fect Solution If you're not in the mood for lap sitting and I am, may I suggest that we compromise? Let me get my human lap fix for a spell. Then perhaps you can let me sit near you rather than on you. (I will be quiet.) Remember the karma thing: What goes around comes around. Chances are, there will be a time (whether you're sick or well) when you will crave a fur fix and I may not want to share my warm and fuzzy body with you—but I will. (I promise.)

Pet Peeve #37
Hogging the Bed

For biological reasons, we crave warm sleeping quarters, too. Therefore, we like to sleep close to our humans. It's bothersome to us when you sleep diagonally—it's confusing. We like to sleep on a warm and comfy bed, preferably yours, but if you don't keep your body in a vertical position it's difficult to choose between your head and the pillow. Worse, we end up having a catfight over space in the bed. Not fun.

Purr-fect Solution   We need to compromise. Let us curl up by you (in a vertical position, please) and try to get along. Do this for thirty days. It should become a habit. If you let us sleep with you, we may purr you to sleep (and you won't need any other sleeping aids). But caution: Purring cats at bedtime can become addictive.

Feline Tip   If you won't sleep with me, perhaps a T-shirt with cats on it will make you feel closer to me as I find somewhere else to sleep. Cat T-shirts are available at specialty pet stores.

Pet Peeve #38
Kicking Me Out!

If you let us sleep on the bed and then push us out, it's inconsistent human behavior. By kicking us out of your bed, you're making a statement: *It's my bed.* Your territorial behavior can make some of us have a hissy fit. After all, we like a cozy oasis, too. Just make up your mind. Either we get to nuzzle up to you in the bed or we don't.

Purr-fect Solution Cat-bed makers take advantage of the instinctive feline desire to be hidden and safe. A potpourri of cozy, soft, and plush bedding is available—some with high sides shaped like tunnels, some that resemble egg crates, and others that look like A-frame houses or igloos. But note, we make good bedfellows because we don't snore.

Personally, I prefer to sleep on my human's bed. (I have learned to deal with the water in it.) In fact, I have gotten her so trained that I hear her calling my name, Kerouac, each night to come to bed. But for hygienic reasons—such as an aversion to fleas—some humans prefer that we sleep in our own beds. (See Pet Peeve #24.)

Feline Tip Inviting cat throws, anyone? Toss a warm blanket complete with different types of cats on the bed and we may or may not sleep on it. Cat blankets are available at specialty pet shops.

Pet Peeve #39
Day People

Let's face it: Our sleep schedules clash. You try to get seven to eight hours of shuteye during the night. We are morning larks and night owls. Ever notice that we like to bat around our cat toys or swipe a paw at the dog when you are trying to fall asleep? Either way, your lights are out by 11 P.M. and that puts a damper on a cat's "midnight munchies," or 6 A.M. food cravings. (Despite the nocturnal label that has been hung on us, we are actually crepuscular, which means we are more active at dawn and at dusk.) What's more, I don't understand why humans don't respect our daytime power naps. Jealousy, perhaps?

Purr-fect Solution So if our pitter-pattering through the house at odd hours disturbs you, turn to water squirt bottle behavior modification. (I prefer soft pillows tossed my way; it's a fun cat–human pillow fight.) Oh, and about demanding meals at odd hours? If you leave for work at 8 A.M., don't feed us until 8 A.M. In other words, by not reinforcing our eating at odd hours, you teach us to abide by your time clock. (Please do not send your cat's hate mail to my publisher.)

Feline Tip If our hours continue to clash with your sleeping schedule (and people point out that you always look tired), it's time to go to a plastic surgeon, retrain me, or go to a pet shrink.

Pet Peeve #40
Unable to Understand Felinese

While we can learn to adapt to your sleep schedule, it would be nice if you got a handle on Basic Cat Talk 101. Because frankly, if you don't get my cat sounds, you won't get me. It's like being in a foreign country and unable to find a person who speaks in cat. Ugh! Think about it. After a while, if nobody can understand you (no matter how hard you try to communicate), it becomes annoying, right?

Purr-fect Solution Tracy McFarland, D.V.M., The Cat Doctor in Santa Clarita, California, comes to the rescue. She has translated our six most frequent messages to you (or other cats):

- Meow ("meooowwll"). Our most common cry, used when we're hungry, lonely, cold, or just want to say "hello."

- Hiss ("hissss"). A sharp, whispering snakelike noise that shows discontent and hints to "back off!"

- Moans ("mmmm"). May be a low, mournful cry, which is an indication of displeasure, pain, or a desire to flee.

- Caterwaul ("awhool"). A shrill, discordant cry often made by toms on the prowl or if a cat is in heat.

- Purring ("purrr"). A soft, vibrant sound to show contentment, anxiety, or even discomfort.

- Yowling ("yeroowwll"). A loud, mournful wail or cry used when discussing territory with a neighborhood cat or indicating disorientation to old age or loneliness.

Pet Peeve #41
Reading My Mind

If you just halfheartedly try to understand our innermost cat thoughts, it can be worse than not understanding us at all. The problem is, people who don't totally open their eyes, heart, and mind to us will not be able to understand why we are thinking what we think. It's not fair to us or you. And it can be oh-so draining, especially if we have to teach you how to do it.

Purr-fect Solution Hook up with a translator, or "pet psychic." These folks can help you learn how to communicate with your cat by making a psychic or telepathic communication with us. You can talk to us through your images, sounds, and feelings. Animal communicator Sonya Fitzpatrick, for example, offers these tips to help get you started: Begin with a calm mind and a calm atmosphere. Say our name telepathically to get our attention. Visualize us as you say our name. Ask us if there is anything you can do for us. Always acknowledge the answer, whatever you get back from us. And remember, trust your imagination.

Feline Tip For information about the wide world of pet psychics, go online and type in "pet psychics." You will find animal communicators such as Fitzpatrick, who provides workshops and phone consultations; log on to her website at www.sonyafitzpatrick.com. Also try www.animaltalk.net/consultlist.htm and www.cyberark.com/animal/communic.htm.

Pet Peeve #42
No Cat Toys

I can't imagine a world without cat toys—nor would I want to. Toys are the way to my heart. And if I have to do without them I'm going to have to resort to scratching the furniture or swinging on the drapes to release my pent-up cat energy. I can't help it. Please don't personalize my playful-aggressive cat behavior. (My vet calls me a "young athlete.") If we can't play with cat toys, what else can we do for fun?

Purr-fect Solution Cat toys amuse me. Toys bring out the wild cat in me. I can chase feathers, bat balls, and pounce on a mouse that makes funny noises. Life is worth living with cool stuff like this. And indoor cats, like me, need mental and physical stimulation or we will climb the walls (literally speaking, of course).

Pet Peeve #43
The Wrong Cat Toy

We come in all ages and have different personalities. Chances are, if you don't know your cat, you will get the wrong cat toy and experience a sourpuss. A few months ago my human brought home a hideous toy mouse that rattled. It was as big as a rat. I refused to play with it. She said, "Don't you like your new mouse, Kerouac?" Duh! Uh–*no*. I was an unhappy camper because that rat thing was not my fantasy. She knows bite-sized fur mice cat toys are my thing—but I've de-tailed all of mine, and the new shipment hasn't yet arrived. (See Pet Peeve #44.)

Purr-fect Solution To get some hints about what your cat really wants, home in to your pet's personality. Observe. Is kitty outgoing? A homebody? To get a clue about what we want, here is a quick guide. (I fit into all five "cat"-egories):

- Social Puss. Interactive toys that tempt us to chase, pounce, and leap with you are good choices.

- Hermit Cat. Toy furry mice and state-of-the-art balls are super because we don't need anyone to play.

- Spoiled Feline. Plush toys such as an extravagant multilevel cat tree are best, since we love to be pampered.

- Sporty Kitty. Objects such as fishing pole–style doodads or wind-up toy mice will urge me to stalk and move.

- Lazy Pussycat. Forget interactive gadgets—too much work. Anything that I can toy with without lifting a paw will suffice.

Feline Tip To learn more about my behavior and compatible cat toys, check out your local bookstore and read up on specific cat breeds' likes and dislikes.

Pet Peeve #44
Not Fixing My Fave Toy

The only thing worse than getting the wrong toy is finding out that our favorite cat toy is out of order—and no one seems to care. Imagine: You are a cat with a specific toy on the brain such as a touch-and-sound-activated rodent that moves when it's meowed at. Then one day it doesn't spin or zigzag anymore. ("Mmmm.") Yeah, we get upset just like humans do when their DVD player or computer doesn't work.

Purr-fect Solution Often cat toys are battery operated. So it's just a matter of getting our humans to pick up a package of batteries (check to get the right size). And if it's not a battery problem, please run, don't walk to your nearest pet store, or go online and put my order in to be delivered ASAP. (I won't stop yowling until my fave toy is back in my paws.)

Pet Peeve #45
Being Catnipless

During those toyless moments, a little catnip could help keep me cool. It irks me when you think that I should go without. Do you think that cats can get addicted to catnip? There are worse addictions, I'm sure. Personally, I can take it or leave it. After all, it is just a happy herb that can make cats roll over and purr. But being catnipless makes a cat crave it. It's like we want what we can't have.

Purr-fect Solution Catnip can be an amusing diversion from life's daily hassles, such as a barking dog or rain. It's not costly. And some cats like it. Catnip comes in all different forms. You can buy it in a bag and sprinkle it on my cat scratch post. (My human said that her past cat companion, Gandalf, used to fall asleep with his paws around the post.) Or you can find it already in some scratch posts and cat toys.

Feline Tip The active ingredient in catnip is nepetalactone, which may or may not affect our nervous system. (Obviously, in Gandalf's case it did not.)

Pet Peeve #46
Bossy Humans

Snippy people and independent cats don't mix. It's a bad combo. Ever try to tell a cat what and when to something? It's useless—a mere exercise in futility, at best. We don't like to be told what to do. It's not our style. Personally, I'll walk away or look at you like you're crazy. Because the fact remains, cats are leaders, not followers. And note, we just don't follow orders (like the dog) unless we feel there is a good reason to do so. Who's the boss, anyhow?

Purr-fect Solution If I am in the mood, I can be complacent and will allow you to tell me what to do. No biggie. For instance, if you shout, "No! Stop eating my plant," I may cool it and jump at your demand (for the fun of it). But if I am having a bad hairball day—save the human orders. I will simply ignore you.

Pet Peeve #47
Absurd Pet Tricks

Independent cats don't do pet tricks upon command. It's an insult to our feline intelligence. "You can't tell cats to do anything. They're in control. They decide whether they want to perform for you or not. It's a cat's nature," explains Dial-A-Vet Sheree Stern, D.V.M., of Los Angeles, California. "Dogs are more wanting to please people, whereas cats want to please themselves."

Purr-fect Solution You've got three choices: One, you can teach self-serving cats, like me, to do dog tricks (yeah, right). Two, you can fetch the dog, who will eagerly perform upon demand. Or three, you can accept the fact that I'm a real cat.

Feline Tip If you want to see a cat do silly tricks, get your paws on Dr. Seuss's classic book *The Cat in the Hat* (Random House, 1966). Amuse yourself—and not at a real-life cat's expense.

Pet Peeve #48
No Cat Parenting Classes

Some folks, especially bossy ones, just don't get the "raising a cat" thing. Once humans realize that we cats are fur children, the cat–human relationship becomes a lot stronger. It doesn't matter what age I am; if you don't have time and patience for me, I will cry. ("Meooowwll, meooowwll.") Yeah, my nonstop meowing will get on your nerves. Trust me on this one.

Purr-fect Solution Make sure we are taken care of . That means when you are busy, keep us occupied with educational cat toys and cat videos. (See Pet Peeve #87.) To share your world with a furry feline child (despite our independent reputation) takes time, energy, and catlike patience. But hey, our stages (such as the "terrible twos" and "teen years") are less difficult than those of human kids. And note, happy cat "parents" share their cat stories with other happy cat parents.

Pet Peeve #49
"Bad Cat!" Words

Using "bad cat" words is not part of good cat parenting. It bothers us to hear you scream "Go away $#!@!" or "Stop that you $#@!." We don't like loud noises and I, for one, certainly don't like mean words darted in my direction. Like most felines, I am a sensitive creature. There must be a more humane way that you can express your ill feelings toward my "bad cat" actions.

Purr-fect Solution If you wish to talk to me about something that you're unhappy about, let's have a cat chat. For the record, I'd appreciate it if you would lower your voice and talk in a civil manner. It's called cat respect. Plus, yelling at me won't enhance our feline–human bond. (If you have any problems, refer to Pet Peeves #40 and #41.)

Pet Peeve #50
Unwanted Water

No! Not w-a-t-e-r! Next time you use that spray bottle and squirt us while shouting, "No Kitty!"—think twice. Remember, most of us have a water phobia (unless it's a faucet dripping). "The tendency for cats to not be big fans of water is something that has evolved over the centuries," says pet shrink Mary Burch. Personally, I can't get forget the image of the anti-water witch in *The Wizard of Oz*. Okay, I may be a drama kitty here, but water is not a cat thing.

Purr-fect Solution If you know that squirting water keeps Kitty from scratching your stereo speakers or hanging from the drapes, do it, if you must. ("I'm melting!") But can't we try another type of cat "correction"? Next time I turn to "bad cat" behavior, let's have a cat chat. Or how about a kitty diversion? Bring out that fave toy of mine and ask (don't demand) me to play with it instead. (Dry cats can send their thank-you notes to my publisher.)

Pet Peeve #51
Anti–Pet Shrink

If we get squirted with water one too many times, it may send us over the edge. Just because you are annoyed when we yowl 24/7 or exhibit catty aggression toward our feline roomies doesn't mean we're crazy. Like humans, however, we may need a little professional help to get us through a rough patch. So if a shrink can help humans, why not cats? It's not fair to make us hold in our "bad human" feelings.

Purr-fect Solution An animal behaviorist can help us get through those pesky human dilemmas. This is our chance to solve what is really bugging us. Think of a pet shrink as a go-between who can help keep order in our happy home, especially in the long term.

"There are going to be more indoor cats for survival's sake. By moving them indoors, however, you're going to have other cat-related dilemmas. There may be some spacing problems if people move from bigger houses into small apartments," points out pet shrink Dr. John Wright. "So you're going to see more cat-to-cat aggression and cat-to-person aggression. As a result, people will be using animal behaviorists more to cope." P.S. Pick up a cat behavioral book or do research on the Internet before you make an appointment with a pet shrink. That way you'll have a clue about our problem.

Feline Tip The American Veterinary Society of Animal Behaviorists (AVSAB) has a list of animal behaviorists who have a D.V.M., M.S., or Ph.D. in animal behavior. Go to its website (www.avma.org/avsab) and contact the secretary-treasurer.

Pet Peeve #52
Dumping Me at the Pound

You didn't take me to the pet shrink, did you? It's not fair. How would you feel if your family gave up and left you at a place for unwanted humans? No matter what you think, it's not fun for us. Despite our chances of getting a new home, we will sit in a cage and play the wait-and-see game. (Been there, done that.) Worse, if we had a strong human–cat bond with you, we'll probably yowl to express our loneliness.

Purr-fect Solution Before you fly off the handle, toss us in a crate and whisk us off to cat prison, *wait!* May I suggest placing an ad—"Cat needs loving home"—in the newspaper? Or perhaps you can pass the word around to cat-friendly people that I am available. (Traitor!) But please, do your homework to find me a cat-loving home. Psst! Give them this book as a cat-warming present. Or if you read it, you may have a change of heart.

Feline Tip An estimated four to six million cats and dogs are killed in shelters each year. Millions more are abandoned, only to suffer from illness or injury before dying, according to The Humane Society of the United States, *Pet Overpopulation Facts* (1999).

Pet Peeve #53
Starving Me (Sort Of)

Some show cats must make small sacrifices. According to cat show expert Marva Marrow of Los Angeles, California, "For those of us with cats that need to have 'tubular' and not *tub*-ular bodies for the shows (I have Oriental shorthairs—they fit into the tubular category), the adult cats cannot have breakfast so they won't look like boa constrictors who have just swallowed a boar. The cats would love to get fed—*lots* of food—but have to wait until the end of the day."

Purr-fect Solution The adult cats do get to graze by getting little bits of food throughout the day, adds Marrow. She says, "Licking the little spoon with the baby food on it is like caviar for a cat, though." Personally, I'd pounce on the fish delicacy—and hold in my tummy.

Feline Tip To appreciate the bold and beautiful show cats, access show calendars by logging on to the allpets Community/Resources section at www.allpets.com/community. Or check out the Cat Fanciers' Association' (CFA) website to get an up-to-date list of upcoming CFA cat shows around the world—www.cfainc.org.

Pet Peeve #54
Fussing, Fussing, Fussing

Show cats are primped a lot. "The fluffy-type cats are literally combed, poked, prodded, fluffed, sprayed, fluffed again, moussed, powdered, brushed, and combed to remove the traces of powder. *All* day long! The shorthaired breeds are slicked down with a chamois and whisked in the ring," explains Marrow. I think I can hear their hisses of disgust as I write.

Purr-fect Solution Humans can help their show cats learn how to meditate. If their haven is on a sunny deck, in the woods, or in some other calming place, just let Kitty get comfy. Dim the lights and put on some soothing tunes. Kitty can do some deep breathing and visualize that cat-friendly peaceful place, one that can put a cat in a relaxed mood. Bring snapshots of Kitty in a happy spot. Creative visualization is free and can prevent a trip to the pet shrink.

Feline Tip For more de-stressing cat advice, go online and check out pet shrinks such as Isabel (www.catshrink.com), who knows all about show cats' likes and dislikes.

Pet Peeve #55
Ignoring Me

Imagine: You're a show cat and the show doesn't go on. You sit and sit and sit while the judges have gone AWOL. No doubt, pretty pusses frown upon being transplanted from their comfy benching cages to the cold judging cages. "*Then* some judges decide it's break time while show cats are sitting up there, bored, ready to party on the judging table, with cold air from the overzealous air conditioner blasting right down into the cages," says cat spokesperson Marrow.

Purr-fect Solution It would be nice if things ran in a timely fashion at cat shows so that the uptown cats could strut their stuff and be done with it all. If they could just make a cameo appearance and then go back to their benching cages, it would be purr-fect. "*Or* . . . put the longhaired cats where the wind blows, put the short-haired cats where the heat is going full blast!" adds Marrow.

Feline Tip Let a show cat hear some tunes for amusement. To order the *Music for Cats and Kittens* audio CD, go to the website www.romeomusic.com/funforcats.

Pet Peeve #56
Anti-Cat Lodging

Show cats and non–show cats often aren't allowed in show hotels. If you can find cat-friendly havens, your cat will be in heaven, sort of. The downside, according to Marrow: "The air conditioners are too noisy. There is no refrigerator to explore. And everyone is always telling us '*Shush!*'" Personally, as a recluse I'm not sure if going out to *any* hotel or motel would make me want to stretch out my paws and purr.

Purr-fect Solution However, cat-friendly lodging may do the trick. Marrow gives her show cats' inside report: "It is really fun having all that attention in the hotel. Room service is *great* and it is *really* fun to lick those individually wrapped little tubs of butter." Pet-friendly motels are less expensive than four-star hotels. Either type may require a security deposit.

Feline Tip Pet-friendly lodging is not new, and many hotels such as Holiday Inn, which are located worldwide, do allow cats. Also, the staff will help plan your pet route if you are traveling with your cat. For more information, log on to www.6C.com and go to link Plan Your Route.

3. Heart and Soul Meows

Pet Peeve #57
Gossiping About Me

Ever notice how cat people will blab about their cat's very personal details with another human? For instance, my human will use a third-person narrative while whispering to a neighbor. "Kerouac was a bad cat today. I caught him shredding my chair." Uh, Hello. I'm right here. We get the message, sort of. "Cats learn to associate cue words with actions," says Wayne Hunthausen, D.V.M., director of Animal Behavior Consultations in Westwood, Kansas. Cats, like me, don't have to be rocket scientists to know that when you're pointing to a chair and cat that you're tittle-tattling. ("Hissss.")

Purr-fect Solution I'm asking for a little cat respect here. For starters, the stronger the human–cat bond, the more we understand you. Rather than tell the whole world that we pooped in your fave plant—save it. Nosy people don't need to go there. Please don't dish out intimate details about us, your beloved cats, especially when we can understand, sort of, what you are saying. Let the cat have your tongue. Or be a sweet-talkin' human.

Pet Peeve #58
Being Disregarded

Imagine how we feel when we come up to you and you don't acknowledge our presence. It's humiliating. We think it's rude. John Wright, Ph.D., a certified animal behaviorist in Atlanta, Georgia, and author of *Ain't Misbehavin'* (Rodale, 2001), agrees. "The cat has invited an interaction" he says—and that's a big deal for us. It's an insult to me, personally, if you pretend I am not in your face when I know that you know that I am indeed present and seeking attention.

Purr-fect Solution Whenever cats, like me, greet you it's a surefire signal to stop, look, and listen. Then acknowledge our presence. It's an instant feel-good message. If you're busy at the moment (seriously busy), will you leave a cat-related message on the answering machine? Turn the volume up and call in regularly. This will be more humane than acting clueless and catless when we get in your face.

Feline Tip If you're going to be out of touch for a while, consider hiring a cat-sitter. Check the Yellow Pages for petsitters in your area.

Pet Peeve #59
No Space

While I don't want to be ignored (like most cats), I do need my space. If I'm in my fave spot, back off ("hissss!"), because as the famous actor Greta Garbo once said, "I vant to be alone!" It also irks me when I'm scoping out the bird outside or hanging out in a new spot and I get a human intrusion. It ruins my whole cat trip. I took the time to get my groove and I want to keep it.

Purr-fect Solution Says animal behaviorist Dr. Michael W. Fox, vice president of The Humane Society of the United States in Washington, D.C.: "A lot of cats like a secure place, outside of regular traffic. Some will like a spot with a view. Other cats like to get up high, like on tall pieces of furniture, because they feel more secure." The bottom line: You need to know when to give us our private time. A sign that reads DO NOT DISTURB should do the trick. Hang it next to us when we are unavailable.

Feline Tip Consider getting a backup cat such as a very vocal and doglike Siamese to keep you company.

Pet Peeve #60
Waking Me Up

Not only do we like our space, we love our sleep. We are big sleepers. Fit adult cats spend about 15 percent of our lives in deep sleep, 50 percent in light, or slow-wave, sleep, and 35 percent awake. You do the math. Nothing bugs cats more than humans who move in on us and disturb our cat dreams when we are taking a catnap. Worse, reality bites if we're happily stalking imaginary mice in our dreams and the chase is interrupted by you. Go away.

Purr-fect Solution Although nobody knows why cats spend twice as much time sleeping as most other mammals, we do. Some experts believe sleep is an overnight battery recharge that allows the body to rebuild tissue and replace spent cells. The idea here is simple: Let sleeping cats lie.

Pet Peeve #61
Not Waking Me Up

On the flip side, if something "cat"-aclysmic happens, abort Pet Peeve #60 and wake us up! We need to know what's going on in your world. It bothers us when something happens and you don't let the cat in on it. If we happen to be in a snoozing mode during a Kodak-cat moment (such as when a house mouse scampers by) don't count us out. We're family.

Purr-fect Solution   Brainstorm: We both can wear matching collars with a noisy bell, like some humans make cats do. Next time something of cat interest occurs, you will likely get up to check it out. When your bell jingles, you will automatically think of me. Just find me and whisper, "Kitty, wake up." Or if I am nowhere in sight, give me a holler and my bell will lead you to me. It's a win–win situation.

Pet Peeve #62
Bumping Me

It's no surprise that sleeping felines (or awake ones) have their fave hangouts. Being booted out of our place is like a human being evicted. It ticks us off because you're violating our Kingdom, says Dr. Wright. We work hard day and night to find those special nooks and crannies (whether it's on your computer desk or the kitchen countertop). So, when you push me out of my place, it hurts my fragile feline ego, and it doesn't do my cat body any good, either.

Purr-fect Solution We choose our fave cat spots because they have scents that we like, warmth from the sun coming through a window, or something cool that catches our eye, says pet shrink Dr. Mary Burch. "Think about why the cat is choosing this space. Once you've figured it out, you may be able to help the cat choose another preferred spot." But note: We are persistent, and we are territorial. (I love being on the computer table and swiping the monitor screen. Why should I give that up?)

Feline Tip Kitty sills and cat trees (especially in sunny spots) are a trade-off that may—or may not—entice us to get off or give up our perfect place.

Pet Peeve #63
Baby Talk

Being bumped is one thing, but when strangers come up to me and start that coochie-cooing thing—help! I mean, how would you like it if Mr. or Ms. Nobody came up to you and cooed, "Oh, look at you. My, my. What's your name, little one? Coochie-coochie." Excuse me, I am a dignified cat, not a baby. We aren't happy campers when the coochie-cooing starts. We think, *Most people talk to me in a normal voice. Why is this strange lady making these sounds to me?* Explains Dr. Burch, "Cats don't know how to respond to a stimulus that is as unfamiliar as strange-sounding baby talk." She's got that right.

Purr-fect Solution Ask your friends (especially the ones I don't know) to nix the baby talk when they're in my presence. Ask them to just talk to me in a normal tone of voice. But note, if you are the party guilty of baby talk, that's cool. We've got a one-on-one thing going on. For instance, in the film *The Truth About Cats & Dogs,* Janeane Garofalo stars as Abby, a single woman who hosts a popular talk show for pet lovers. During one memorable scene, Abby talks to her feline Babyhead and coos: "Can I have a kiss? You didn't kiss me when I came in, sweetest of all sweet cats in the world. Thank you. Thank you my lovely."

But caution: Watch what the cat does when you speak baby talk. "If the cat responds to baby talk by coming and getting in your lap for petting, it's okay," says Dr. Burch. That means we, like Babyhead, are digging it.

Feline Tip According to the 2001 AAHA Pet Owner Survey, 78 percent of the 1,209 respondents said they talk to their pet in a different voice.

Pet Peeve #64
Being Your Shrink

Speaking of baby talk . . . Cats are purr-fect sounding boards. We listen and keep it confidential. Plus, we are nonjudgmental. But frankly, when you whine about your work, love life, and health woes, it does get a bit overwhelming. Can you give it a rest—perhaps on Sundays? Cats need to regroup in order to maintain that cool and calm composure six days a week. Hey, you're getting 24/7 counseling sessions here.

Purr-fect Solution I will continue to listen to you if you will acknowledge my cat talking and body language. For example, next time I scratch the walls to alert you to the fact that "I'm hungry," feed me instantly. Just act on my actions and I will be there for you, as always. Fair enough? FYI: A human shrink can charge $120 an hour; cats don't charge, yet.

Feline Tip According to the 2001 AAHA Pet Owner Survey, 52 percent of the 1,192 respondents claimed that their pet listens to them best (even better than a spouse/significant other, family member, friend, or other).

Pet Peeve #65
Not Sharing Meals

If you share your life's most intimate details with us, why won't you share your breakfast cereal? It's okay for you to spill your guts to The Cat daily, but if I dip my paw into your milk you shoo me away. I don't get it. What if I just ran away next time you get a craving for me, the cat sounding board, to listen to your caterwauling about taxes or the next-door neighbor?

Purr-fect Solution If I get to share cat morsels of your meals (my choice), I will be there for you always like before. No increased rates. I will listen to you (like a good cat) if you promise that you'll cut me in on the good eats. Waste not, want not.

Feline Tip Ceramic cat bowls with cat faces (a cute reminder for you to share with us, your free sounding board) are available in selected specialty stores.

Pet Peeve #66
Banned From the Fish Tank

Why do you have a hissy fit when I pounce on top of the fish tank? Don't you want me to lower my blood pressure, too? Hey, if it works for humans, it must have a healthful effect on felines. And yeah, we cats have stress, and watching the fish keeps us on an even keel.

Purr-fect Solution If you let me have rights to the fish tank, I vow not to terrorize the cold-blooded fishes anymore. I'll just look. Sooner or later, the fish will be desensitized to my furry cat face and whiskers as I stare into the glass tank. Plus, fish tank–watching is free. This is a good release for indoor cats, like me. Also, if new-and-improved cat toys are out of the question due to lean times, I see no other alternative.

Feline Tip Check out a computer store in your area and inquire about screen savers with fish tank themes.

Pet Peeve #67
Putting Your Work First

What if I, your beloved pussycat, put the fish tank before you? That's how I feel when your work is number one and I come after. Okay, I know you bring home the fish. But hey, all work and no play makes you a very dull person. Plus, I should come first. Why? I don't have to answer that. (I am a cat.) But you know that we are whimsical creatures. And when you put all of your energy into The Job, it really gets to be a bit of a bore.

Purr-fect Solution Give it a rest. No kidding. Whether you're a telecommuter (like me) or go to the workplace, you've got to take breaks and get your priorities in order. Repeat: "Family comes first." Rather than tune us out, tune in to us. We've got that laid-back attitude down to a fine art. And we are centered. Let me be the center of your life. But caution: Don't take too much cat time off from your work, because we cats have to be provided for. (Translation: We need food, treats, litter, toys . . . You know the drill.)

Pet Peeve #68
Human Arguments

If the vacuum cleaner frightens me, imagine how I feel when humans are screaming at each other. We can't handle it when you argue with a significant other or a family member. It even upsets me when you yell at the dog. Any tiff disturbs my tranquil space. If you're not willing to lighten up, cat behavioral problems may rudely affect our peaceful roost.

Purr-fect Solution   You can keep me calm by making our household as stress-free as possible. Try to resolve relationship issues together. If I act like a frightened child, make some changes. Therapy for you ASAP may be helpful. If you nip your problems in the bud, I won't need a cat shrink, which will cost extra. And note, if my peeing on your fave garment or hiding in the cupboards is starting to worry you, it's cat therapy time.

Pet Peeve #69
Divorce—Who Gets the Cat?

While we don't like heated arguments, divorce can turn the cat's life into a topsy-turvy world. Yeah, it does affect the cat when the marriage bond is broken. During this high-anxiety time, we feel the chaos as we watch our families split apart. "Everyone recognizes the potential impact of marital distress on children, yet the effects of family dysfunction on household pets have been swept under the rug," says pet shrink Dr. John Wright.

Purr-fect Solution Animal experts can help pinpoint signs of high anxiety (such as improper elimination and hiding) and reduce feline stress. We are sensitive creatures and sense when you are going through a mixed bag of emotions. It will help to deal with our turmoil or we may go AWOL and you'll have another problem: POW kitties.

Feline Tip For $1.50 plus tax, rent the film *The War of the Roses*. (I have to put my paws over my eyes during the scary pet scenes. Poor Kitty.)

Pet Peeve #70
Cataclysmic Events

Before, during, and after a breakup or terrible disaster—tornado, hurricane, fire, or earthquake—we may behave strangely. Some people say it's ESP (extrasensory perception), or a sixth sense. Personally, I can't tolerate it when narrow-minded humans roll their eyes when I start to act chatty or clingy or hide under the bed. It bothers me a lot, too, when humans think our sensitivity to change is a laughing matter. Perhaps cats don't sense danger, says Dr. Wright, but we do sense, and react to, a change in routine or environment. And sometimes we'll act out and run over and over an escape route or make noise to get outdoors.

Purr-fect Solution Since scientists admit they aren't able to 100-percent reliably predict tornadoes, hurricanes, or earthquakes, go ahead and monitor my strange behavior. Perhaps together we can up my prediction success rate. Rather than buy expensive electronic equipment, cats are cheaper and may even be better when it comes to earthquake prediction and hurricane and tornado forecasting.

Feline Tip Check out "Lost and Found Animal Reports" on the Earthquake Prediction Online website at www.syzygyjob.net.

Pet Peeve #71
Scary Sounds

Like quakes, loud noises that go bump in the night (or day) are on my blacklist, too. If I hear a mysterious sound, you're on your own—I'm out of here. "Being afraid of loud noises is a survival skill that has kept cats around for centuries. Running for cover when you hear something that is obviously much bigger than you is actually a smart thing to do," points out Dr. Burch.

Purr-fect Solution Whatever you do, stay cool. "Act like everything is under control," recommends Dr. Burch. Just chill and it will help us sensitive kitties get through it—no matter what "it" is. That means if we're weathering an F4 hurricane or Killer Bees, you be the rational one. Fake it if you have to.

Feline Tip Rent classic disaster movies such as *Earthquake* and *Twister* and we can watch them together. It will desensitize us so we'll both be cool cats if the Big One hits.

Pet Peeve #72
Natural Disaster Unpreparedness

I know we get kudos for sensing imminent quakes. But hey, what if a fire or flood strikes, and you're not home? I'd freak out! I never said I was Supercat. Sure, I can jump out a window. But what if the windows are all shut? What am I supposed to do? I don't know how to call 9-1-1. (Perhaps that is one cat trick I will allow you to teach me.) I can't handle being alone during and after a "cat"-astrophic event.

I've heard my human talk about the Oakland Fire. On Sunday afternoon, October 20, 1991—just two years after the Loma Prieta earthquake rumbled through the California Bay Area—a devastating conflagration created a Stephen King–type nightmare for East Bay pet people and their cats and dogs.

Purr-fect Solution So plan ahead. Here are some tips for your cats, straight from the disaster services of The Humane Society of the United States (HSUS).

- If you split, do not leave me behind to cope.

- I should wear a collar and up-to-date I.D. 365 days a year.

- I need a backup plan in case you aren't home when disaster hits. Contact cat-friendly friends and family members now to ask if they would be willing to get me and meet you at a pre-arranged place.

- Find out where we can go together or board me for temporary housing. Most emergency shelters will not allow cats.

- Pack a disaster kit for me that includes food (my favorite, please) and water, bowls, leashes, carriers (don't forget Mr. Blanket!), a list of phone numbers, vaccination records, my re-quired meds, cat litter, and a cat box. (Keep a spare on hand. You know how finicky I am.)

Feline Tip Get a pet alert decal and stick it on a front room window. If there's a natural disaster, rescue workers will know if I am a trapped kitty. To get a free emergency decal, write to St. Hubert's Animal Welfare Center, P.O. Box 159, Madison, NJ 07940.

Pet Peeve #73
Rodents That Get Away

It's another disaster if we don't catch our prey. After all, the ancient Egyptians were so devoted to us, and prized us so highly for our rodent-killing ability that killing a cat was a crime punishable by death. We can't tarnish our rat-busting reputation. It's not fun for a twenty-first-century house cat to find—and lose—a live mouse indoors. But rodents that get away can be even worse for the feral cats who need to catch them for survival, especially in the winter. In my neighborhood, for example, I saw a young cat (not more than one year old) waddling alone outside. She was obviously very pregnant and very hungry. It saddened me. It made me recall our last snowstorm. During the night I listened to the cries and catfights of feral kittens underneath our house. (Actually, that's how I was found as a kitten.)

Purr-fect Solution For indoor wild cats at heart, like me, find the best imitation toy varmint possible. This way we can have our mouse and eat it too (so to speak). And with state-of-the-art rodents we can play Cat and Mouse and always catch our prey. It will make any pampered feline feel like a wild cat.

Feline Tip Speaking of wild cats . . . Trap, neuter, return (TNR) for feral cats is a progressive and positive program offered by some shelters and agencies to help prevent the cruel pickup and kill methods. For more information, go to the Alley Cat Rescue website, www.saveacat.org.

Pet Peeve #74
Forgetting My Birthday

While too much holiday chaos can make a cat hiss or flee, not celebrating our existence can drive us mad. I watch you throw human
birthday events and pooch parties. I don't complain. But honestly, it
gets my goat when nobody pays attention to me.

Purr-fect Solution Cats enjoy their humans celebrating them.
It makes us feel important. You can join me in my fave activity, make
a special cat-safe birthday cake or treat for me, and sing happy birthday, too. Also, a gift-wrapped present (lose the unsafe ribbon) is welcome. Cats aren't materialistic or party animals. A can of gourmet
cat food and a cat toy will suffice.

Feline Tip According to the 2001 AAHA Pet Owner Survey, 675
respondents said they celebrate their pet's birthday by participating
in their pet's favorite activity.

Pet Peeve #75
Fourth of July

While honoring my birthday is important, loud parades, parties and fireworks can frazzle my feline nerves. Because I'm sensitive to chaos, Independence Day can be one of the most dogged days of the year for me. Did you know that missing-cat reports soar with the Fourth of July observance? Sudden excitement, noise, and change frighten cool cats and make us want to pull a Jack Kerouac and hit the road. Check to see that my cat I.D. tags are up to date.

Purr-fect Solution As you get in the patriotic spirit, I'll start my deep breathing exercises. Here's are some holiday survival strategies to cat-proof my Fourth of July:

- A few days before America's Birthday bash, when I start cringing and fleeing at the sound of booming fireworks, pay more attention to me. Keep me indoors—day and night—despite my yowling. Desensitize me to noise before the holiday. Try playing some music at a low level. Then slowly increase the volume each day. The result? I'll associate noise with happy times. Go ahead—treat me to the luxury of a quiet room. Also, fetch that soft and plush blanket or comforter (you know the one) to provide extra security.

- Once D-Day arrives, I'll be in my "quiet room" with a big sign posted on the door that says FOR CATS ONLY! Visits are allowed by you or familiar folks. But please, don't make me be a nice kitty to the party people. Tell them that I've got a headache. Meanwhile, keep the holiday sweets (especially chocolate, which can be toxic) and alcoholic beverages away, too. Do not leave decorating supplies (ribbons, balloons, confetti, tape, or scissors) around me, either. And never light sparklers, firecrackers, cherry bombs, or any fireworks around me.

- After the fourth, don't leave used fireworks where I, the curious cat, can get to them. And don't assume that the day after the Fourth of July is safe. (There are cases of abuse linking fireworks and cats.) Perhaps, after the dust settles, you can treat me to a postholiday party. A calm and quiet evening with my favorite cat chum and fish treat will do just fine.

Pet Peeve #76
Halloween

While the Fourth of July is frightening to cats, Halloween is not safe for us to roam free on, either. Halloween is the one holiday on the Satanic calendar that scares me to the max. Spooky reports of ritual cat mutilations always increase around October 31. No wonder Halloween is on a cat's pet peeve list.

Purr-fect Solution   If possible, put me in a crazy costume so humans will not be able to recognize that I am a cat. It will help me to avoid Halloween goblins. Don't assume that because we are not all black (personally, I have white on my chest and paws) that we won't be picked up for sacrifice. All colors are sought. The choice often boils down to the first easy mark. Report any suspicious activity involving pets in your neighborhood to 9-1-1 immediately. Do not let me outdoors—day or night.

Feline Tip   Use extreme caution when selling or giving away my fellow cat friends during the Halloween period. If possible, don't do it at all.

Pet Peeve #77
Thanksgiving

No doubt, cats are more suited to Turkey Day than to ghosts and goblins. Still, there are some glitches even on this day. We cats, like humans, anticipate the big bird while it is washed, dressed, cooked, and served. How can we resist?

Alex, my human's past orange-and-white cat companion, couldn't. Once the big bird was cooked and placed on the dining room table, he moved in. As the story goes, when his human and her family members were out in the kitchen, that bold cat snagged that tasty 15-pound bird and fled like a wild cat with his prey.

But according to the AAHA, if we get our paws on turkey leftovers, we can fall victim to salmonella (an organism that hides in the bird's tummy) food poisoning and other food evils that are nothing to be thankful for.

Purr-fect Solution To prevent me from getting sick because the big bird is undercooked or has been sitting out at room temperature too long, don't let me have a chance. However, during your turkey feast, please be sensitive to our cat cravings. You don't have to count me out. Just make up a special kitty plate.

Feline Tip To preorder Thanksgiving cat treats, seek out online specialty pet shops such as Pet Celebrations. (See Pet Peeve #172.)

Pet Peeve #78
Christmas

The ongoing holiday season can make me switch from nice to naughty. I'm ultrasensitive to change, chaos, and crowds. The holidays can drive me up a wall. Don't be surprised if I act in some unmerry ways (such as scratching the furniture or hissing at your guests). The holidays can also bring unexpected dangers for us because of too much attention or, on the flip side, not enough of it.

Purr-fect Solution Here are some cat-savvy tips straight from Dr. Wright to help keep me cool:

- Protect me from too much attention. A lot of pats from new people can get my goat! Let guests know that if I want to be petted, I'll come to them, says Dr. Wright.

- Stick to routines. Even though your schedule may be topsy-turvy right now, try to keep my mealtimes and playtimes the same.

- Create a safe holiday. We can hurt ourselves if we play with tree trimmings or decorations. We require tricky work, like placing breakable figurines on high shelves that leave no room for a landing.

Feline Tip Give me a treat- and toy-filled Christmas stocking and I will forgive you.

Pet Peeve #79
A Houseguest

It's upsetting if your guest is hyper or someone we don't know. If it's an unknown human, I have to be on guard: See the cat in high places or low spots. Like other cats, I'm uneasy around new people because I'm a territorial puss. Plus, unexpected company can interrupt my impromptu catnaps.

Purr-fect Solution You can help a houseguest get a warm cat welcome if you introduce us slowly and properly. Don't force me to be an affectionate cat (even though you know and I know that I can be one). I will nudge up to Aunt Emily or Uncle Fred if and when it feels right. But let the houseguest understand that I need the vibe to feel right before I play friendly cat.

Feline Tip Some people cats will befriend any two-legger, be it a good neighbor or bad burglar.

Pet Peeve #80
No Houseguests

Zero humans or animal visitors, however, can make a social cat want to find a more happening home. If you deprive us of social interaction, we can get bored. I like people and cats. I crave interaction. It can make my cat day. So if you are a hermit crab (like my human) take note: We cats get lonely if nothing new comes or goes our way. ("Yeroowwll.")

Purr-fect Solution Cat people must understand that socialization is good for both of us. Yes, I mean let's both rub elbows (paws in my case) with some people. I like cerebral longhaired cats and humans, myself. Indeed, mellow cat-friendly felines and people who have something to share intrigue me. If we don't have visitors we will end up too isolated and go psycho like that Norman Bates character.

Feline Tip Some cats, such as the introspective Persian, can take or leave houseguests.

Pet Peeve #81
A Feline Roomie

Cats also have trouble adapting when their humans bring home another puss without getting their cat's pawprint of approval first. Personally, I could handle a feline fur fix—as long as I remain Kerouac, the Top Cat. And note, if a new cat tries to pull rank some cats, like me, will not remain a purring machine.

Purr-fect Solution Make the introductions slowly. You can keep the new cat in a crate for a spell. This will allow us to get used to each other's scent and sight. After a while, when the vibe is right, go ahead and let us meet one-on-one with human supervision. Do this a few times in short intervals and then give us a time-out. Sooner or later, the chances are that we will either become soul mates or tolerate each other.

Feline Tip If you want to save a cat life, consider rescuing a feline, which will cost less than buying one from a cat breeder and will make a homeless cat's day. (Visit your local animal shelter for a variety of cats from which to chose.)

Pet Peeve #82
Your New Mate

A new cat is one thing. But a new mate for you would be like me opening up Pandora's Litter Box. Once we open it up, who knows what will happen next? As you can tell, I, Kerouac, am a people cat. But when a human brings home a potential significant other, it can be a rude awakening. We cats may feel jolted and jilted. After all, we are territorial, and a new human, especially in the initial stages, may be a threat to our peaceful kingdom. It's like a box of cat treats. We never know what we're going to get, like Forrest Gump's wise mom said.

Purr-fect Solution Easy does it. If you must unite with another person (I thought I was your one and only), we can adjust if you do it s-l-o-w-l-y. Don't toss a new two-legger into our household without proper introductions. Invite your mate to share quality time with you and the skeptical cat. It takes a while for us to warm up to a new person, but we can come around.

Pet Peeve #83
An Anti-Cat Mate

If your significant other isn't a cat person, I will not be jumping for joy (nor will you). We have an uncanny sixth sense when it comes to knowing when we are welcome—or not. If I act clingy or restless or even flee, you can bet that I'm not happy with your choice. We cats can pick up clues quickly that a man or woman is fearful or unsavory. "If your cat has a track record for sniffing out bad people or users, go with their sixth sense," says Mark Goulston, M.D., a Los Angeles, California–based psychiatrist.

Last winter my human invited an anti-cat man over. She said that he liked cats. In her dreams. At first, I scoped him out like a lion stalking its prey. We were not the fun-loving trio on *Three's Company.* To my human's surprise, after she spent "quality" time with this dog man, her world turned topsy-turvy. He left her like a tomcat. I stayed and licked her tears. Meanwhile, my romantic "mistress" and I hope that a real cat-loving man such as Charles Dickens, Albert Einstein, T. S. Eliot, or Mark Twain will saunter into our lives and we will live happily ever after.

Purr-fect Solution While cats know best, if you're unsure about our judgment, wait. It may take a while for us to chill. And remember, we can be jealous and territorial. So during your courtship stage, spend extra quality time with your beloved pussycat. And with patience, we may warm up to the two of you—or not. Pssst: Pick up a stray cat for me. This way we can find out faster if your new mate is potential cat people—or not.

Feline Tip Connect with cat lovers by placing an ad in the personals. (This can be done on the Internet or in a newpaper.) Mention that you are a devout cat lover.

Pet Peeve #84
Too Much Novelty

Houseguests, mates, anti-cat mates—aaahhh! If it starts to feel like a scene out of *Animal House,* we will be out of sight. Too much new stuff can put cats, like me, in stress-overload mode. Cats can make mountains out of molehills when one new thing enters their lives. Imagine how we feel if two or three changes are made all at once. It's just too much for most cats to handle. And don't be surprised if we fly the coop if life gets too hectic. Remember, we are self-reliant creatures and can fend for ourselves.

Purr-fect Solution Take inventory of what's going on in our household. If it seems like people are constantly coming and going (and you're getting complaints from the neighbors), there may be too much novelty at home. Think *less traffic, more quiet time.* In other words, think like a cat. What cat in his right mind would enjoy constant doorbell rings, loud music, shouting, catfights, and chaos? Act more like a cat and you may find that you can keep yours at home.

Pet Peeve #85
Car Rides

Most cats, like me, do not like to jump into the automobile and play Go Cat. We are not dogs. Also, if we're in the car, chances are, we're going to the vet. This is a double whammy that can stress out a feline to the max. It's like we're moving into an episode of *The Twilight Zone* or *The Outer Limits*—a point of no return. ("Hissss.")

Purr-fect Solution I guess we'll have to get in the automobile sooner or later. We can do it the easy way. When we least expect it, pick us up and place us in the crate. Then place a towel or blanket over the crate (it makes us feel safer) and put us into the car. Soft words and reassurances such as "This is only temporary" and "You will get through this" may make the journey less frightening. Yeah, right.

Adds Dr. Burch: If you don't wish to use a carrier, an alternative way to teach a cat car-riding behaviors is to have a helper. "If you are the cat's favorite person, then you need a driver for the cat–car rides training program. The driver does the driving and all you worry about is acting calm, dispensing reinforcers (treats, pets, and praise) and letting Kitty know that everything is okay."

Feline Tip Some cats on the big screen (such as Harry's Tonto in the classic man-and-his-cat film *Harry and Tonto*) do like going on the road. But that is not real life. Plus, cat actors get paid to do it.

Pet Peeve #86
Not Picking Me at the Pound

Taking our freedom away sucks. Imagine: A cat sits in a cage. One by one, strangers ogle the live ball of fluff and poke their fingers at the animal. If Kitty doesn't purr, the show is over. This is the tragic scenario cats face every day. Of course, being trapped is a pet peeve all cats dread, fear, and hope will never hit home. How terrible to be one of the homeless felines in the world.

Purr-fect Solution Since I came from a rescue shelter, I know firstpaw what it is like not to have a family of my own. When I was chosen, it was a scary ordeal to be transported to an unfamiliar place. But after two days, I discovered that being the chosen one has cat perks. If you see a cat in a box at a shelter or rescue group, open up your heart and arms. You can change a cat's life. This is another Kerouacism.

Pet Peeve #87
Home Alone

Giving a cat a home is cool. But some cats (especially active ones, like me) get bored if we are left home alone too long. It's true. For instance, I like it when my human (and the dog) are home. It makes me feel safe and secure. Plus, if I want company while I play, eat, or sleep I have options. But when I am home alone it gets too quiet. I don't like it. In fact, one of the neighbors told my human that she heard me scratching on the front door. Duh! I was lonely. ("Yeroowwll.")

Purr-fect Solution Since cats, like me, can be self-absorbed and arrogant, pet-sitters are the ultimate answer to scratching off this pet peeve. "These pampered creatures are going to be upset if you don't make arrangements to replace their human with a pet-sitter who will try to outdo you in servitude and entertainment," says Patti Moran, president/founder of Pet Sitters International in King, North Carolina.

If you can't afford a real cat-sitter, putting on a video just for cats may be the next best bet for spoiled pussycats. It may be a cat's dream-come-true. If I can watch birds, butterflies, and living creatures chock-full of sounds, I will be amused.

Feline Tip For more information, go to the website www. cattv.com/VideoCatnip.htm. This cat video, for example, provides twenty-five minutes of birds, squirrels, and chipmunks designed for your pampered kitty to watch. To order, call (800) 521-7898.

Pet Peeve #88
Middle-Cat Neglect

Speaking of lonely cats . . . Ask yourself these five questions—for your middle cat. If you answer yes to more than two, add middle-cat neglect to your cat's potential pet peeves list.

- Am I forced to seek affection from the dog rather than from my human?

- Does my human play with the firstborn cat more than me?

- Were my humans shocked when I had a litter of kittens?

- Do I run away when my human attempts annual cuddle time?

- Has my human forgotten my name?

Purr-fect Solution If you can find your middle cat, it's time to regroup. Schedule play periods for your cats and try to initiate play that meets each cat's individual needs. Plus, if you neglect your middle cat, you may start to see attention-seeking behaviors (for example, nonstop meowing) or territorial responses (such as litter box mishaps and squabbles).

Pet Peeve #89
Smothering Me

Being the firstborn or only cat can have its flaws, too. Listen up: Kerouac will give you the inside scoop on the downside of being the solo feline. You give us applause for every purr and sandpaper tongue lick. Sure, the attention is cool, at first. But come on now, it's like Big Brother is watching my every move. I can't even use the litter box without getting rave reviews from my human and the dog. ("Hissss.")

Purr-fect Solution No doubt, the number-one cat, like me, is exposed to lots of new sounds and sights. That's cool. It will make us more laid-back—well-adjusted cats. Good human! But it's equally important to let us experience stuff solo. Cats need breathing room. It will help enrich our cat–human bond if we don't smother each other. Read: I enjoy doing some cat things alone.

Pet Peeve #90
Playing Favorites

But note, solo cats, like me, may become tigers when a newcomer visits or enters our family and you give them more of your time than you do me. Hey, I know I was just caterwauling about too much attention, but when a cat's order in the family is jeopardized, we can have a catfit. And chances are, if you start to favor a new pet or human—watch out. King Kerouac–type cats will roar loud and clear.

Purr-fect Solution   Simply put, avoid playing favorites. Why? You'll also avoid territorial responses such as squabbles and litter box mishaps. Or we may flee if we are demoted. Again, cats are independent creatures. And if we are treated unfairly, we will seek attention elsewhere. This is not a threat. It's a promise. ("Hissss.")

Pet Peeve #91
Moving

Hierarchy to cats is a big deal, but moving is an even bigger event. Moving is a grueling *Grapes of Wrath* road trip. Cats don't like traveling or change. Uprooting and plopping a cat into a new and unfamiliar environment is scary. Cats can sense a move way before it occurs. From when you first discuss The Move to when the first cardboard box is filled, we sense that something just isn't right. Personally, I flee under the bed when the word *move* is brought up.

Purr-fect Solution Okay, here's the deal. If you're planning a major move, keep it hush-hush. Talk about it out of the household so I won't have to hear about it. Spare me the gruesome details. Then you can move on to plan B of your covert operation. Either pack up slowly: Take one picture a day down, move a pile of books near the door—step by step (it may take months). This way, we may be fooled and think that you're just rearranging our house. Or on D-Day (perhaps a day before) put me in my fave room. Then yank it all out at once—like a bad tooth. This way I won't feel the pain as much. (However, I bet most cats would rather have a root canal and stay put.) And cat people know that it's a pain to move the cat, too. "People get into a panic if they don't have enough medication for their pet, no appropriate documentation for travel to other countries, or money to pay for border fees," says Dr. Walt Ingwersen, an AAHA vet in Whitby, Ontario. "Be prepared by bringing a copy of your pet's medical records, proper documentation and medication, and knowing the laws going into the new city or country."

Feline Tip For more information on moving with your pet, go to the AAHA's website at www.healthypet.com.

Pet Peeve #92
Cat Ageist Attitude

If I don't like change, I won't like growing old, either. Worse, I can't handle catty digs about the feline aging process. It's unacceptable human behavior. As I age, I will be less frisky and, perhaps, more cranky. But cats, like me, don't need you to point out the signs of growing old. Insensitive comments such as "Fluffy's coat isn't what it used to be" or "Felix can't jump up high anymore" irritate me now and must bug senior felines to the max. ("Hissss.") Boy, I'll bail (even if I am hobbling with a cat cane) if I hear phrases like this when I'm a senior cat.

Purr-fect Solution It's important to us that our humans adopt a hang-in-there attitude when we have a senior cat moment. It's part of cat life. We need you to be there for us. Actually, growing old with you by our side can be romantic. Uh, that reminds me while my memory is good. You know the toy fur mouse gifts that we bring you? If we are ever disabled, please return the favor—breakfast in bed would be nice.

Pet Peeve #93
Not Getting Our Nine Lives

The thing that bothers me more than a cat ageist is a nonbeliever in our amazing nine-lives phenomenon—the uncanny ability to bounce back. It frustrates me when humans give up and let us go too soon. By not believing in our nine-lives cat thing, you may pass up a cat miracle.

Purr-fect Solution My human gets the nine-lives thing, and you can, too. It happened without warning on an autumn night. One moment her eighteen-year-old, gray-and-white cat Gandalf was resting; the next moment he lost control of his hindquarters and fell to the floor with all four legs rigid. Rather than let her bounce-back cat go, she sought help . . . One vet visit later plus a few prayers, her senior cat was alert and vocal. Two days later, Gandalf was on the road to recovery and back home. Now that's a four paws up to our nine lives!

Pet Peeve #94
Not Letting Me Go

On the other side of the coin, our nine lives will eventually run out. Come on—nine lives is a lot. As a pampered cat, I know how intense the feline–human bond can be. And, yeah, it is hard to call it quits. Remember, I—like all cats—am persistent. But our bodies give out before our souls do. Thus, there comes a time when we have to say good-bye.

Purr-fect Solution If I am ailing and you are uncertain if it's time to bid our farewells, may I suggest seeking professional guidance? Sometimes one vet's point of view isn't enough. Get a second opinion. Perhaps a pet psychic can help you make the final decision that we can live with (or in my case die and be content about it). Also, if you are in touch with my cat spirit, follow your heart and I will guide you.

Pet Peeve #95
No Life After Me

Ever notice that once you make the decision to let go, you may act like a fickle puss and change your mind? Cats understand. However, we also realize that once we go, life goes on. Wouldn't you feel silly if you found out that we were having the time of our lives, either in Kitty Heaven or back on Earth as a dog? (Scratch that. A bird.)

Purr-fect Solution When the time is right, please fill the cat void. Personally, I can handle being replaced by a new cat. It's flattering. It will help to recall the good times we shared. Don't forget, stray cats are free (in case one is roaming your neighborhood). And according to cat lore, having a stray cat in your home is a sign of financial improvement soon to follow.

Feline Tip If grief is a problem, visit a comforting website. For example, www.petloss.com offers pet-related chat rooms and grieving rituals.

Pet Peeve #96
Not Taking My Ghostly Calls

After-life cat tales may also be a factor for cat people to consider. After we die, we may choose to have a telepathic reunion with you. Cats hate it when you don't answer. For instance, if you're lying in bed and you feel our little feet pitter-pattering on you, it's a sign for you to feel our after-death presence. It's rude if you don't acknowledge us. ("Meow.")

Purr-fect Solution "Many people can feel their pet's energy," explains animal communicator Raphaela Pope, coauthor of *Wisdom of the Animals* (Adams Media, 2001), "even though they know their animal has passed. Sometimes they are lying in bed and can actually feel little feet leaping on the bed." Also, if you see your furry feline friend in a dream (especially six to eight weeks after the loss), don't be scared. This isn't uncommon, either.

Feline Tip For $1.50 plus tax, rent the video *Ghost* (add $2.00 for kitty treats). Watch the movie with your live cat and see how people can have telepathic reunions with their loved ones.

Pet Peeve #97
Insisting I Come When You Call

Indeed, when you say "Come here, Doggy," the mutt will be in your face pronto. We cats, however, have our own agenda. Ever hear the lyric "Now if you need me, call me" from the classic song "Ain't No Mountain High Enough"? It bugs me that you would even consider insisting that I come upon command. We are independent cats—not needy dogs.

Purr-fect Solution "Cats live to please themselves. You can't tell or make a cat do anything," points out Dial-A-Vet Sheree Stern. Once you accept the simple fact that we are cats—not people-pleasing dogs—life will be perfect. We will come to you, but it will be on our own timetable—not yours. As for that song . . . I've made a minor revision for cats: "I'll be there when I get there." (Don't hold your breath.)

Pet Peeve #98
Being Tagged Anti-Social

Just because I don't come at the drop of a hat doesn't mean I am a recluse 100 percent of the time. Sure, I have moments when socializing is not going to fit into my cat day. And true, I'd rather sun myself on a warm windowsill or stalk a bird through the window than have a cat–human heart-to-heart. (It is annoying when you invade my private time.) But just because I can act nasty like Jack Nicholson does in *As Good As It Gets* when the dedicated novelist's sacred writing schedule is interrupted, it doesn't mean that I can't be social. I can be a people cat and cat cat—sometimes.

Purr-fect Solution Hear me out. (I'm feeling social now.) Understand that we are ambiverts, which means that we can be social *and* anti-social, depending upon our mood and what time of day it is, of course. The upside is, you get two cats for the price of one. But note: Check with me before you include me in any social cat events. I will have to check my calendar and get back to you.

Pet Peeve #99
Demanding Affection

The fact remains, we semisocial pussycats detest having to give affection upon command. That's the dog's job. I, for one, will be doting when I feel like it. Just back off and let me come to you. Please don't demand that I cuddle, nudge, and make butter (knead my paws) on your lap. I will do that mushy cat stuff, but it has to be on my terms. And the more a human demands affection, the more we will pull away. Cats can't tolerate being forced to dish out cat love.

Purr-fect Solution Since I will give my cat love to you, it's best to understand how I do it. Some people believe the cat who licks you reveals mega amounts of affection. Others insist love is in our eyes. "When a cat blinks both eyes slowly at you, that's the equivalent of a human blowing a kiss," says Dr. Tracy McFarland, "and the expression of deep contentment and comfort for you."

Feline Tip According to the 2001 AAHA Pet Owner Survey, 39 percent of the 1,197 respondents said they rely on their pet for affection in their family.

Pet Peeve #100
Making Me Perform for Treats

If you crave cat affection, why would you ever ask me to perform for treats? Just the mere idea has spoiled my appetite. It's silly that you'd expect me to "sit up" or "sit down" upon command. (See Pet Peeve #47.) I am a cat with attitude. We are not stupid or lazy. We can do these things when we want to do them—not when you want us to impress dog people. The treats are an embarrassment. Get real. I'd rather starve.

Purr-fect Solution On the other paw, I know how much it means to cat people to be able to show off their feline's IQ. I find this touching. So, personally, I will do dog tricks on special occasions. (I really want to learn how to dial 9-1-1.) But ask me (begging gets extra points) to perform a task and the odds are fifty-fifty that I will comply. Please, save the kitty treats and corrections for the dogs. It's just too humiliating.

Pet Peeve #101
Telling Me to Act Like a Dog

If cats don't do dog tricks, then why would we want to act like a pathetic pooch? It gets my goat when I hear people say, "Nice cat, but he isn't a dog." Duh! Why would I ever want to be a subservient canine, anyway? Barking and wagging my tail just isn't my thing. If you think that cats will change and act like the world revolves around you, forget it. That's the dog's job. I'm not interested. Please, it's an insult to my cat smarts.

Purr-fect Solution If you want a dog, get a dog. But if you already have me in your life, it will be best (for both of us) if you accept me as is. I am a sassy feline with a strong mind of my own. I am independent, intelligent, and fickle. I am Cat. I can be affectionate, calming, and your best friend—if you let me be me. I need to take a nap now. Don't you have something to do? ("Hissss.")

Now that we've discussed cats, let's talk dogs. ("Meooowwll.") . . .

PART TWO

Your Canine's 101 Pet Peeves

(From the Dog's
Perspective)

4. Body Growls

Pet Peeve #102
Food With Killer Chemicals

I've heard from my pet pals that chemicals found in some commercial pet foods may increase cancer risk, cause liver damage, and shorten a dog's life span. Personally, I would never flush out a sick bird to feed you. Even though dogs are known to eat anything, if we knew the facts about some dog foods (the ones with unhealthy chemical additives, preservatives, and artificial flavorings), we would not put them on our daily dog menu. ("Grrr.")

Grr-eat Solution I am sitting up and begging you (for all the good dogs in the world) to dump the fake stuff and turn to an all-natural or more healthful pet food. In other words, hunt and gather high-quality and minimally processed dog chow without fillers, sugar, or chemical preservatives.

Canine Tip Whatever you decide to buy, check to see if the label on my dog food reads that it is formulated to meet the minimum nutritional standards set by the Association of American Feed Control Officials (AAFCO) Dog Food Nutrient Profile for maintenance.

Pet Peeve #103
No-Name Kibble

While brand-name commercial-base food containing killer chemicals can be bad, generic dog kibble is worse. Ever notice how those brown tidbits sit in our dog food bowl? Even the cat turns up his nose at it. The reason: It looks and tastes bland. Of course, if we have a Great Depression I will eat it—for survival's sake.

Grr-eat Solution A good way to keep dogs, like me, youthful and healthy is by feeding us a high-quality or premium natural commercial-base food. That means dishing up a dog chow that bears a known name, such as Iams or Hill's. These dog foods contain all-human-grade ingredients and are preserved with anti-oxidants like the heart-healthy E and immunity-boosting C.

Canine Tip According to the 2001 American Animal Hospital Association (AAHA) Pet Owner Survey, 83 percent of the 1,214 respondents ensured their pet's quality of life with premium brands of pet food.

Pet Peeve #104
Zero Junk Food

While my athletic dog body craves premium-quality natural chow, with a brand name, life without junk food is boring. Like you, I too crave a slice of pizza or a cheeseburger. It hurts my dog feelings when you devour fun fare in front of me and say, "No, Dylan. It's mine." How selfish is that? As a pack animal, I would share my prey with you.

Grr-eat Solution Once in a while, a piece of all-natural veggie pizza (with a whole wheat crust and extra veggies) won't kill me. (Hold the anchovies, please.) The best part is, we will share these forbidden foods together and it will enhance the canine–human bond. Meanwhile, I will work on my begging style to help convince you that no human junk food is a bad thing.

Pet Peeve #105
No Home Cookin'

Let's discuss another mega gripe—no home-cooked meals for dogs. Please don't underestimate our canine smarts. We know you prepare home-cooked food. Ironically, while our chow is in a bag or can, we watch you fix a fresh meal that includes protein, whole grains, raw veggies, and healthy oils. But what I don't see is why we dogs can't eat good food like that. It's downright inhumane.

Grr-eat Solution If you really want to make us happy and healthy, take the advice of holistic vets (the docs who consider our total well-being). Let us in on the healthful home cookin', too. Because it's rich in vitamins, minerals, fiber, and living enzymes (good for my digestion), it'll support our health and help to boost our canine longevity.

Canine Tip There are prepared home-style dog food brands available at a variety of stores.

Pet Peeve #106
Not Feeding Me on Time

Once you get the hang of dog-style home cooking (and my tail wags), don't forget that we are creatures of habit. When doggy meals are served late, our sixth sense kicks in. We know something is wrong. If dinner is not on the floor, like usual, it upsets us. Ever notice how dogs will pace before it's chow time? Our motor drive kicks into motion, naturally. We can't help it. It's our way of telling you that we prefer to be fed at the same time every day. We don't like our feeding schedule changed.

Grr-eat Solution If I bark to alert you that it's feeding time, please see this as a positive cue and don't reprimand me. This way, if you're busy you will have one less thing to remember. But you will have one more thing to do—feed me. If you're going to be late, please make arrangements with a dog-friendly neighbor or petsitter so I won't become light-headed.

Canine Tip Consider investing in one of those automatic dog feeders, such as the product available from Quick Feed at www.quickfeed.com. (No barking required.)

Pet Peeve #107
No Water Refills

Both food and water are key for our health. Like fussy cats, we prefer drinking water to be available 24/7, and it's best fresh. If my water bowl is empty (and I am panting overtime), it's a hint for you to refill my water bowl. If not, don't yell "bad dog!" when you find me hanging out at the toilet bowl like sitcom *Mad About You*'s Murray (my hero). Also, exactly why do I get water from the tap? It's not fair that I lose sleep over the deadly chemicals that may be floating in the water you pour daily into my dog bowl.

Grr-eat Solution By fetching fresh water (bottle or distilled), you can rejuvenate us. How? It flushes toxins from our body, and enhances our good health just like it does for humans. In fact, I prefer to lap up that Mountain Spring water that you drink.

Canine Tip Consider investing in one of those continuously running water fountain–type products that cats love. They are good for smaller-sized dogs, too.

Pet Peeve #108
Being Anti–Pet Supplements

While diet and water are a dog's best friends, dietary pet supplements are nice, too. But you ignore the fact that I may need them. You wouldn't think of missing your daily disease-fighting anti-oxidant vitamins C and E. (These help you to stay well and live longer.) It's not fair that you'll take health-boosting supplements and act like we don't exist. By being pro–human supplements and anti–pet supplements, it makes us feel that you're leaving our good pet health in the hands of chance.

Grr-eat Solution To maintain good dog health, holistic vets recommend good-quality, natural vitamins—like the ones you take. If you're thinking of going the cheap route, think again. The synthetic, bargain vitamins and minerals aren't absorbed in my body as well as the good stuff.

Canine Tip You can find dietary supplements at your pet or health food store.

Pet Peeve #109
Overfeeding Me

If you feed us too much, you'll end up hanging out with a corpulent canine. Like humans, some of us pack on unwanted pounds, especially if we're sofa spuds or wolf down too many high-fat snacks. Personally, I'm an active pooch like a typical Brittany (I still weigh in at 42 pounds). But I've seen pudgy pooches and I know (thanks to my health-oriented human) that their body fat is not heart-healthy and can cause other health problems that can decrease a dog's life span.

Grr-eat Solution A healthful diet can keep unwanted dog pounds at bay, but so do other things my human does that help keep me fit and trim in my Golden Years:

- Perform a one-minute weight check weekly. Palpate my lower tummy (rub it afterwards, please). If there's more than 1 inch of flesh, that's a red flag.

- Discover portion control. Our food intake depends on our individual metabolism, weight, age, and lifestyle. Consult with our vet first.

- Take me in for regular preventive vet checkups which help to keep tabs on my weight. The vet makes me get on the scale at every visit.

Pet Peeve #110
No Dog Snacks

I've had Junk-Food Junkie dog pals. They binged on potato chips and fast food. It's not for this dog. Fast-food fixes—laden with fat, caffeine, and sugar—can make me as moody as the cat. Worse, they can make me shake from head to tail because I am a "Shaky Puppy." Years ago I had a scary episode. At first, it felt like monsters were chasing me, and then I was dog tired. My vet tagged me with an "epilepsy" diagnosis and said it seemed that certain foods (such as chips) trigger a shaky event. So I have nixed junk food (like other shaky dogs have done) and I have been standing on steady ground ever since.

Grr-eat Solution Train your human to be a health nut like mine. You'll get low-fat, natural treats, an alternative to human junk food or fat-laden pet goodies—and not have to beg. I get grapes (the purple ones are healthier) and raw almonds (I love the crunch).

Pet Peeve #111
Boring Stuff

While being a health nut is cool for canines, we still crave doggy delights from bagels to cinnamon rolls now and then. It's inhumane to lick ice cream and gulp down pastries in front of us and pretend we can't see you. Check out our intense doggy stare. We know that you know that you're getting comfort by eating a carton of chocolate chip ice cream. And it makes us feel dogged if we don't get any.

Grr-eat Solution You can let us indulge in special all-natural doggy cookies and cakes if you find a doggy bakery. These are utopia-type places where the human staffers offer canine goodies to us for the thrill of it. This way we can have our cake and eat it, too.

Canine Tip Log on to the Internet and search for dog bakeries like Three Dog Bakery. Call (800) 4-TREATS or visit www.threedog.com.

Pet Peeve #112
Begging Me to Hurry Up!

Trying to speed up Mother Nature is stupid for humans and dogs. It's no fun when someone barks at you to "Hurry up!" and finish your business. It makes me want to growl. Not only is it insensitive, but it ruins my concentration. We dislike being pressured during the delicate art of clearing our plumbing. It takes time, patience, and a knack for picking out the perfect place to lift our leg or squat. Important things like this really can't be rushed—nor should they be. It stinks!

Grr-eat Solution The upside (for you) is, "Dogs can be conditioned into going fairly quickly," points out Stanley Coren, Ph.D., professor of psychology at the University of British Columbia and author of *How to Speak Dog: Mastering the Art of Dog–Human Communication* (Free Press, 2000). "The way that you do this is fairly simple. When you start training the dog as a pup, you catch them in the act and attach a word to that. The word that I use is 'Quick.' And be consistent." And yep, this trick works in the rain, snow, sleet, and, well, you get the picture. Speaking of pictures . . .

Canine Tip Take a snapshot of us doing the "Quick" dog trick. Post our photo on the fridge. And remember to allow extra time for puppies and senior dogs.

Pet Peeve #113
Making Me Hold It

Countless indoor dogs, like me, are expected to "hold it" until their human is available to let us go outside. This is a mega pet peeve for canines of all ages. "It's a biological need. No one likes to hold it. Our choice is to either let loose on the rug, which then we'll get heck for, or to endure the pain until Mom and Dad decide to come home," explains pet shrink Dr. John Wright. It's so hard to hold it (especially at my age!). But we dogs do this for our humans to keep the peace.

Grr-eat Solution The way I see it, you've got three choices: Get a doggy door so I can go and come as I please. Buy some kind of dog litter, so I can relieve myself like a cat or toy dog breed. (I'll pass on this one.) Or, if you want your walking papers, make arrangements with a dog walker before you go out.

Pet Peeve #114
Not Scooping It Up

I can be rushed. I can hold it. But I won't be the scapegoat for not cleaning up after my dog business. For dog's sake! I am a canine with four paws. Scooping it up is a human thing, not a dog thing. I can't handle stepping in it. Worse, people who step in dog poop say mean things. Some people with dog authority will post NO DOGS ALLOWED at parks because you didn't scoop it up. Pet Peeve #114 is one that I will not forget.

Grr-eat Solution You can do one of two things: Find an easy-to-use scoop that works on grass or pavement. Or, hire a pooper scooper. I'd opt for the first suggestion unless money is no object.

Canine Tip Pooper scoopers like Doggie Pooper Scoopers, which are made from recycled paperboard, are available at www.scooperdoggie.com.

Pet Peeve #115
"Bad Human!" Dog Walking

While dogs, like me, love to get a move on, inept dog walks are a four paws down. Next time you witness a dog pulling his human down the street, don't smile. Take it from me, Bird Dog, it's no laughing matter. If a dog hasn't trained his human how to walk in public, it can be a drag (literally). It's not our fault that you allow us to walk you in front of the world. This feat of dog tugging human on the street embarrasses humans and dogs worldwide. It makes me want to put my paws over my eyes.

Grr-eat Solution Basic obedience classes can help those humans without prior dog training. It teaches the human how to use basic dog command responses, such as when walking with us on a leash. Also, if we're going to new environments, I like to know beforehand what the dangers are. My life depends on it. Are there aggressive dogs or wild animals? What are the leash laws? I don't want to be hounded by either.

Canine Tip A basic course of obedience classes that teaches humans how to walk us can vary in cost from $75 to $105. The courses are usually six to seven weeks long, with one-hour classes held once a week.

Pet Peeve #116
No Dog Walks

If you don't take me out for regular walks, I'll turn catty. My nonstop barking or constant whining may annoy you. Blame it on no dog walks! I feel so sad when you go out the door without me—Go Pup. I need to stop and smell the roses, too. It's cruel to go in and out all day without me. After all, I am your canine companion, right? If you don't let me get my daily dog fix of fun, I don't want to hear your complaints that I'm too "hyper" or "fat."

Grr-eat Solution It's a two-for-one deal. Teaming up with me increases circulation, burns off fat, reduces stress, boosts energy, and fosters a sense of well-being—for both of us. That means we'll both get the benefits of feel-good endorphins (those natural mood boosters). And in my case as a senior dog, walking can help to decrease the onset of arthritis. Also, let's go to a new neighborhood. Says Wayne Hunthausen, D.V.M., "It's really stimulating because there are new smells and new sights."

Canine Tip If you don't have the time, search the Yellow Pages under "dog walking" and find a human who offers dog walks on a regular or periodic basis. It can run about $14 for one hour.

Pet Peeve #117
Ignoring My Physical Talents

We can't handle it when you ignore our physical canine abilities. Why can't humans take note when Fido jumps 10 feet high in the air? That's your cue to get the dog into hurdling activities. When you ignore our physical gifts, it's an insult and it hurts our doggy feelings.

Grr-eat Solution Check out dog breed books at the library and/or use the Internet to discover what canine activities we are best suited for. Agility (fun on a mind-boggling course with agility obstacles such as hurdles and tunnels), or search and rescue (work that entails finding people and saving them), can excite the right dog breed. For best results, match our breed and age with the appropriate dog activities.

Pet Peeve #118
Weekend Warrior Syndrome

Many humans are weekend athletes. After five days without exercise, you decide to go do it and take the dog. While it's great to get outdoors, I am a sporting dog and can't comprehend what it means to overdo it. However, when I get home after a day of nonstop running and jumping, I understand that I'm sore. Worse, if we both have aches and pains and can't walk, who will take care of us?

Grr-eat Solution Dr. Anne Lazar, an AAHA vet in Lake Oswego, Oregon, recommends starting younger and middle-aged dogs on a moderate walking program: ten to fifteen minutes once or twice per day. This, in turn, will get us both in shape for the weekendfest. For senior dogs, like me, a vet checkup is in order before we team up. And please don't make us run the 10K the first day out.

Here are some great physical activities that dogs and their humans can enjoy together—in moderation:

* Bicycling. Irish setters and Brittanys, who have lots of energy, will love to run by your side.

* Hiking. Weimaraners and Brittanys, who are shorthaired (so maybe Brittanys aren't shorthaired, but we love to hike) and won't pick up brush or stickers in the wilderness, are good hiking partners.

* In-line skating. Golden retrievers and Brittanys (I couldn't resist—I love the outdoors!), who are known to be good runners, have stamina and are usually not aggressive toward people or animals passing by.

* Jogging. Border collies and Brittanys (I couldn't resist), who are known to be runners, have high energy and are ready-made joggers.

Canine Tip So we don't fall victim to orthopedic injuries—which go-getter sporting dogs, like me, can do—hire a cost-effective high school student or senior to walk us daily so we will stay in shape for your action-oriented weekendfest.

Pet Peeve #119
Thinking I'm a Hypochondriac

It bugs me when humans tune out my whining if I feel something is wrong—or could be one day. For instance, if I am limping and you think, *Puppy wants attention*, think again. It may not be in my imagination. It could be real. I will not fake an injury to get attention. (That's the cat's job.) It's irritating when you play the wait-and-see game before we go to the vet. Don't you care about my peace of doggy mind?

Grr-eat Solution I promise not to cry wolf if you vow to take notice of any unusual canine behavior. True, my whining may be due to the new dog on the block. But then again, what if I have a rare doggy disease that destroys a canine in twenty-four hours unless the right antidote is found? (Okay, I may be getting melodramatic here.) Either way, it will pay to tend to me like the folks do to Lassie's cries for help. I'll fetch my leash.

Canine Tip According to the 2002 AAHA Pet Owner Survey, 47 percent of the 1,153 respondents said they would spend any amount to save their pet's life.

Pet Peeve #120
Irregular Vet Visits

Ever notice how vet visits can bring out the fraidy-cat in us? Why the preliminary hassle, you wonder? "Dogs may not like vets because the environment is unfamiliar, or they pick up on the stress and fear of other animals," explains Mary Burch., Ph.D., a certified animal behaviorist in Tallahassee, Florida. Or we may be suffering from post-traumatic stress from a bad experience at a vet's office.

Grr-eat Solution Dr. Burch recommended the following to help make our vet visits (which should be once a year; twice a year for senior pups) more dog-friendly:

- Start me off on the right paw by making vet visits a fun experience.

- Have the staff talk and play with me.

- Bring a towel or my favorite blanket to cover the cold, slippery exam table.

- Ask the vet if he or she would be willing to check me out on the floor. It makes me feel more calm, less threatened.

- Pet me (a gentle massage can be relaxing) and talk to me in a reassuring tone.

- Give me a doggy treat at the end of the vet visit for being a good dog.

Canine Tip According to the 2001 AAHA Pet Owner Survey, 91 percent of the 1,214 respondents said they ensure their pet's quality of life by maintaining regular veterinary checkups and vaccinations.

Pet Peeve #121
Bad Medical Benefits

Okay, so you're all set in case a human medical problem hits. But what about me—the poor dog? What if I get a life-threatening illness or get hit by a car? What will I do? What if the medical expenses sky-rocket and the vet demands cash on the spot? I'm in deep do-do, huh? I don't feel safe.

Grr-eat Solution I'm just a dog but I do know that I can qualify for pet insurance. It will provide coverage for accidents. (You know how klutzy I can be. Remember last summer when I leaped off the hillside like I was Superdog at age twelve?) Pet insurance also provides coverage to help pay for illness, routine care, and annual exams. For more information, contact pet insurance companies to find out about medical benefits.

Canine Tip Consider a convenient phone consultation service such as Dial-A-Vet to answer your health questions, from vaccinations to getting a second opinion for your puppy or adult dog. Call (800) 719-8916. The cost is $24 for the first ten minutes, $2 for each additional minute.

Pet Peeve #122
No Dental Plan

Speaking about health . . . Surprise! We get cavities, gum disease, and chronic doggy breath, just like humans. You go to the dentist twice a year. But what about me? If I don't practice preventive oral hygiene, like you, I may end up toothless or having to wear doggy dentures! (That's a dog's biggest nightmare. How will I chew my bones?)

Grr-eat Solution According to the AAHA and other veterinary experts, the following tips can direct me—your canine companion—toward good oral hygiene.

- Take me to the vet. My vet will do a health checkup that includes a physical and dental exam. If plaque and tartar buildup are a problem, he or she will recommend a cleaning.

- Get a tooth cleaning. A basic cleaning will involve anesthetizing me and could cost $100 or more. Preliminary blood work should be done to indicate whether there may be any preexisting conditions that could complicate the procedure, such as liver or kidney disease. Be aware that some of us (like me, the Shaky Puppy) don't fare well under anesthesia because of allergies, age, or preexisting medical conditions, so ask your vet about this before consenting to a procedure. Once the vet gets your okay, he or she will sedate the dog and do a scaling and cleaning. Consult with your vet regarding how often follow-up cleanings are necessary.

- Brush my teeth at least three times a week. In addition to using a toothbrush, consider trying some newer products such as the Plaque Wacker to fight canine plaque and tartar. Gum disease results from a change in the normal saliva, which creates a buildup of calcium, salts, food, and bacteria that forms plaque on my teeth.

- Use a toothpaste designed for dogs. The foaming agents in your toothpaste will irritate my stomach. Fluoride-enhanced toothpaste also may prevent plaque buildup. They are available by prescription through your vet.

- Feed me a dry food. Dry food fights tartar buildup, and its abrasive texture removes plaque.

- Opt for chew toys. Some good options are rawhide bones and soft rope bones.

Pet Peeve #123
Hiding the Herbs

Regular vet visits are a paw forward, but keeping me away from herbal medicine sets us back. You do herbs. Why can't I? Doing without Mother Nature's wonders can make my life harder than it has to be. If you're feeling blue or think you're coming down with a cold, you reach for herbal remedies. I don't understand why I can't be part of the herbal revolution. It's the twenty-first century. It's not fun being the last dog on the block to take vitamin C or ginseng.

Grr-eat Solution By letting me use herbs when I need them, you will help me stay healthy just like you. Chinese herbs such as ginseng can help enhance my immune system (that's important for a senior dog), and they can also lessen stress (another problem for me, the Shaky Pup). Some herbs such as valerian, skullcap, and oatstraw nourish the brain and nervous system, which may also help prevent Shaky Puppy episodes.

Canine Tip For more information on epilepsy, go to www.yahoo.com and search for "seizures and epilepsy."

Pet Peeve #124
Anti–Alternative Dog Care

As a natural dog, it bugs me when humans give a thumbs down to natural dog care. In fact, when I was diagnosed as a Shaky Pup, the doc wanted to put me on drugs. Yuck. Doggy pills would have zapped my energetic spirit. Worse, what if I had ended up in Doggy Drug Rehab? Bird Dog says drugs and surgery are for the birds unless there is no other alternative.

Grr-eat Solution Like my human, I am pro–natural diet, herbology, acupuncture (if needed), and massage. In fact, dog massage (when a human rubs us from head to tail) is so therapeutic. Trust me on this one. To learn how to do dog massage (dogs would do this for you!), go to the website www.catanddogmassage.com.

Canine Tip For more information about different types of alternative care, log on to the AltVetMed (alternative veterinary medicine) website www.altvetmed.com.

Pet Peeve #125
In the Suds

We don't enjoy looking scruffy and unkempt. But dog baths suck unless they are done the proper way. Our way. Sure, I love to swim. But when it's bath time, it's another story. You can find me in the closet or under the bed. Like other dogs, I don't like to go through the ordeal of being hosed down and sudsed up. It's worse if you send us off to the groomer because it drags out the process. And of course, there is the separation anxiety from our humans. Boy, I'm quivering just thinking about it all.

Grr-eat Solution This bath thing can be turned around into a fun deal if you get creative. Think like a dog. Let's take a bath together like the dog and loving couple do on the TV commercial. I can get in the bathtub or shower with you. Start with warm water, a slow hand, and natural shampoo. Talk to me softly and work your way from my head to my tail—like a dog massage. We can do this. Say "I love you" in between rinsing. Tunes and candles would be nice. Doggy treats, anyone?

Canine Tip If a dog–human bathing session is out of the question, look in the Yellow Pages under "mobile pet groomers" and "do-it-yourself dog washes."

Pet Peeve #126
Inept Nail Trims

This procedure can be so much more grueling than a bath. Years ago I was at the vet for an annual checkup when my mom mentioned a nail trim for Dylan. Minutes later I was tied down and muzzled like a canine Hannibal Lector. Then the insensitive humans clipped my nails, one by one. It was more frightening than watching Cujo, the Saint Bernard, terrorize humans.

Grr-eat Solution These days getting my nails trimmed is okay. My human, like other sensitive dog people, takes me to the same place every month where I am treated with respect. I am not treated like a human criminal or mad dog. No restraints. Nice words. It's a doable experience.

Canine Tip Do it yourself with the proper scissorslike dog clippers and you can save more than $100 a year. Be extra careful not to cut the sensitive vein (the quick) inside the nail.

Pet Peeve #127
No Pest Control

Pet groomers can be pests, but fleas (and other pesky parasites such as ticks and worms) are a dog's worst enemy. We all detest fleas. It's difficult to scratch in those hard-to-reach places.

"Fleas make dogs extremely uncomfortable, and they can cause medical problems," explains Dr. Burch. Imagine if you had a flea (even just one) crawling all over your body, and you couldn't get rid of it. If it bothers humans, just think how it makes us feel. We go doggone crazy.

Grr-eat Solution You can always move to a cold climate and high altitude. Since I have been transported to the California Sierras, fleas are not in my vocabulary. But if moving to the mountains isn't your idea of pest control, you can work with your vet to choose a flea protection program that best meets your dog's needs.

Canine Tip Seek natural ways to control fleas, and use herbal formulas to repel fleas and ticks.

Pet Peeve #128
Unsafe Dog Collars

Dog collars, especially toxic flea collars, are not on my list of favorite dog items. Yes, we can get used to wearing a choker (it helps us to walk you), but that doesn't mean we are big fans of all collars. If you make us wear a chemical-filled collar (to fight fleas), or our collar is too tight or too frilly, it can be a miserable experience. You certainly wouldn't wear these contraptions. Why should we?

Grr-eat Solution Do your homework. Whatever type of dog collar you think will be appropriate, please read the directions. Sadly, most dogs are illiterate. Humans are in charge of getting the collar right. And note: If we drop to the ground, gasp for air, or look shy and self-conscious in front of people and dogs, lose the collar. Find one that fits us to a T and does its job without making us feel like a "bad" dog. Don't even think about those inhumane dog collars to silence our barking. ("Yelp.")

Pet Peeve #129
Stupid Clothes

Dog collars are one thing, but dog clothes? I've seen toy poodles dressed up in doll threads. It looks absurd. My neighbor walks her cute bichon frise clad in a frilly red sweater and booties! I guess it helps keep the white fluffball warm and visible during snow season. But I'd rather freeze. Can you envision me, the senior Bird Dog, wearing a tuxedo? ("Grrr.") I am a sporting canine, not a penguin! For dog's sake! It's a blow to a canine's self-worth. What if my dog friends see me?

Grr-eat Solution Let's compromise. If it's minus ten degrees in the winter a dog, like me, can handle a sporty black turtleneck sweater. But please, save the hats, shoes, and other silly accessories for toy breeds and perhaps festive occasions if you must. If you're even thinking about making dog clothes a daily regimen, make an appointment with a pet shrink.

Pet Peeve #130
Hogging the Bed

Personally, I can't handle it when my human hogs the bed. It gets in the way of my variety of dog postures. I sleep on my back (with four legs up in the air), sometimes I sleep with my head on my paws, and occasionally I sleep on my side. My point is, dogs, like me, will snooze however we want—if given the chance, that is. And more times than not, we like to sleep near our humans, who may not be generous with space. And this can be a problem.

Grr-eat Solution　Let us snooze at the foot of your bed. It makes us feel like one of the pack. Some animal trainers are from the school that says if you allow dogs to sleep with you, we'll think we are equal. You will lose control. That's ridiculous. Next time you hear me mumble, "Hey, move over! I want to stretch out my paws," just grin and bear it. You're the alpha dog.

Pet Peeve #131
Kicking Me Off!

If a dog has been sleeping in your bed and then one day you snap
"Get down" or "Off" (when you are making it up in the morning),
what are we supposed to think? I'm confused. Either you want me
on the bed or you don't. If you flip-flop it hurts my doggy feelings. I
wonder, *What did I do wrong? Are you going to toss me a pillow
and blanket and make me sleep on the sofa like a bad spouse?*
Remember, dogs, like me, are emotional.

Grr-eat Solution However, "Some dogs do like their own particular 'crawlspace.' It could even be a dog crate to sleep in, especially when the human companions are away during the day. It's like
having their own den, which can give a dog a better sense of security," says animal behaviorist Dr. Michael W. Fox, vice president of
The Human Society of the United States in Washington, D.C. And of
course, you probably know that dogs have favorite places where
they sleep (just like humans do), and these may vary throughout the day. Haven't you found your dog snoozing under the table,
by the bed, or in front of the couch? (For dog beds, visit your local
pet store.)

Pet Peeve #132
Lethal Household Cleaners

While kicking us out of your bed hurts some dogs' feelings, pooches like me are also sensitive to a variety of indoor and outdoor environmental pollutants. Dirt, dust, and chemicals can make us miserable. In my case, chemicals can affect my nervous system. That means potential Shaky Puppy episodes, because toxins may irritate my brain tissue. No fun. I can think of better ways to spend my senior years. Translation: Dump the toxins. I don't want to end up exposed to deadly chemicals and be viewed in a *Silkwood* sequel.

Grr-eat Solution I may sound like a persnickety cat, but here is my dog wish list:

- I don't like cigarette smoke, which has too many killer toxins. Have a smoking room if you must—preferably outdoors.

- If you can, use only products with natural fibers (such as cotton sheets) on "our" bed, and an all-natural-fiber sofa would be nice.

- While you're in a redecorating mode, lose the carpets. I just love hardwood floors. (They show my nail scratches better. It's a hint to keep up on my nail trims.)

- Ventilate our house to reduce indoor air pollution.

- And please don't put me in a garage or room (for any amount of time) that contains household chemicals.

Pet Peeve #133
No Doggy Door

Once our house is in order (I sound like a finicky cat, huh?), it won't be perfect until I have my own separate entrance. Like other dogs, I don't like being told "I'll take you outside in a minute" when I want to go *now*. Some cats just jump out a window. And you can come and go as you want. I want the same privilege.

Grr-eat Solution If we have access to a safe, enclosed front or backyard, a doggy door is not an unreasonable doggy request, is it? I promise I will not bark or hop the fence. If I am a good dog, I feel that this device would provide ultimate independence for both you and me. I'm getting excited just thinking about it. It's a dog's dream come true.

5. Mind Play

Pet Peeve #134
Anti-Dog People

Think of *101 Dalmatians'* mean-spirited Cruella De Vil, who is every dog's worst nightmare. Welcome to anti-dog two-leggers. Personally, nothing upsets me more than a human who treats me like a dog. I remember watching abused dog survivors in Jack London's *Call of the Wild* and *White Fang.* Dogs were mistreated in those stories, and they did not forget their abusers. It's degrading. Therefore, if I meet someone who doesn't like me, my tail will go down and I will be on guard.

Grr-eat Solution Beware: Dogs have sharp memories. Use a verbal command to anti-dog people, such as "no!" or "back off," and nip them in the bud. Always supervise interactions between potential anti-dog people and your dog to prevent bad human behavior and smart dog retaliation.

Canine Tip If you think you have a potential anti-dog convert, rent the dog video classic *Old Yeller* and adopt a puppy to sit in the person's lap. If this doesn't do the trick, kick that person out the doggy door.

Pet Peeve #135
Teasing Me

Anti-dog people and dog teasers are of the same breed. Both types of humans make my fur stand on end. Dogs, especially sensitive ones like me, don't like being taunted or made fun of. For example, back in the San Francisco Bay Area I met an anti-dog man who pretended that he was going to share his steak with me. He didn't. Then he had the nerve to act like he was going to kick me off my sofa! I thought, *Excuse me, but I live here—you don't.* His dog teasings continued for a short spell until my human dumped him like a piece of dog poop on the sidewalk. I got the last laugh.

Grr-eat Solution If you witness a human teasing a dog (such as poking a stick at us or barking bad human words at us), please don't walk away. Report these "evildoers" (with all respect to President George Bush). You must fight the war against dog terrorists.

Canine Tip For information on different dog breeds and their temperaments, visit the website www.akc.org and find profiles of each of the American Kennel Club's recognized breeds.

Pet Peeve #136
Unsupervised Infants

For starters, dogs who share homes with new infants may think *I thought I was the baby!* So when a new addition to the family arrives, it can make us feel left out, unwanted, and demoted in the pack order of the household. To a pooch who was Top Dog, this isn't going to be a fun thing. We may feel jealous and curious. And this new bag of mixed emotions plus a new baby can make us unpredictable.

Grr-eat Solution While we are working out our feelings, we need you to be there at all times. It will make us feel part of the family and safe. If baby gets too excited and screams or cries, it will be better if you are there to make both of us feel like this is normal. And note, please supervise us because if my tail is grabbed I, like other well-meaning pooches, don't want to accidentally (on purpose) snap. ("Yelp!")

Pet Peeve #137
Toddlers Who Think We Are Toys

Infants are naive, but toddlers can be taught that I am a real dog, not a stuffed animal. Personally, I don't like it when kids want to play and I don't. If a child bangs on my body like I am a drum or saddles me like I am a horse, it's a terrible ordeal. Hello—I am a live dog here. ("Grrr.")

Grr-eat Solution Kids need to be told that when I want to stop playing, they should respect my need to walk away and regroup—doggy-style. Please teach your children that I like to be petted but not too much. And let them know that my tail (mine is docked) and my ears (mine are the pendulous kind) are not silly decorations. Children need to understand that we take our appendages (which are communication devices) seriously.

But note, I have heard my human talk fondly of her childhood dog–child relationships. Tales about Casey, the high-energy dalmatian, amuse me. The story about her Norwegian elkhound, Ole, made me want to howl. He ran away one day—and she went on an amazing quest to find him (the warmhearted furry friend of her dreams). Three weeks later Ole, the wayward dog, pulled a *Homeward Bound* and reunited with his family.

Canine Tip Toddler-friendly dog breeds include the collie, dachshund, and pug.

Pet Peeve #138
No Hugs

If we dogs pounce on you and don't get hugs, cuddles, and tummy rubs in return, it will make us feel like homeless animals. Human affection provides instant gratification. And if we don't get hugs, we will feel jilted and jolted.

Grr-eat Solution Yours truly often teams up with my human to play couch potato and watch television. (I prefer the Animal Planet channel.) It makes me feel wanted. "It's also good for satisfying the normal social needs that dogs have as pack animals," says Jeffrey Masson, Ph.D., a Berkeley, California–based psychoanalyst who wrote the book *Dogs Never Lie About Love* (Crown, 1997). As you do with your human family, schedule "quality hugging time" with me. It will strengthen the dog–human interaction and help to maintain a healthy emotional bond. Not to forget, of course, lots of praise, petting, and hugs will be uplifting to both human and canine spirits.

Canine Tip For information on dogs and the human–animal bond, check out the Delta Society's catalog of publications. To order, call (425) 226-7357 or (800) 869-6898.

Pet Peeve #139
Pampering You, Not Me

It would also be a nice gesture if you would pamper us the way you pamper yourself. It's not fair that you get to go to plush hotels and outdoor restaurants and have photo sessions without us. I am a fun-loving dog, remember? Please take me with you. I love to be spoiled, too.

Grr-eat Solution The doggone fact is, yes, you can take us with you to dog-friendly places and we can both be pampered. Some plush four-star hotels will allow dogs, and we can get room service. Photo sessions with just the two of us (I personally have done this) are "in," and a pet-friendly photographer can make it an unforgettable experience. You ought to see how he captured the twinkle in my eyes.

Canine Tip For more information on ways to pamper your pooch, check out *DogGone,* a bimonthly newsletter providing "fun places to go and cool stuff to do with your dog." A subscription costs $24 per year. To order, call (888) DOG-TRAVEL.

Pet Peeve #140
Disturbing My Dog Dreams

Sleeping and dreaming are part of my pampering time, too. Although we generally dream during rapid eye movement (REM) sleep, also known as dream sleep or deep sleep, we (more than cats) exhibit signs of wakefulness during this period. What's more, if you observe me wagging my tail or yipping and growling in my sleep, it's quite possible I'm having a dream and it will irk me if you wake me up. Hey, I could be chasing the bird of my lifetime and you will ruin it all.

Grr-eat Solution When you see us paddle with all four limbs (this behavior, along with vocalization, suggests that we are dreaming of the so-called chase), let us be. What if I am one leap away from catching the rabbit? Also, if my dog sounds during REM sleep are caricatures of normal barks, howls, and yelps—chill. But, "The most characteristic physical indication of REM sleep is a sudden burst of eye movements," points out Dr. Michael Fox.

Canine Tip Dr. Fox cautions that if you do decide it's a good idea to comfort us, take extra care since I may be scared or disoriented, especially if I am having a bad dream after a dogfight or injury.

Pet Peeve #141
Not Understanding Dogese

During waking hours it's annoying when humans can't read our canine sounds. It bugs *moi* when Lassie's people understand what her whining means but in real life people are clueless to my dog sounds. I bark, whine, howl, and growl for different reasons, and it's frustrating if these are ignored. It takes a lot of energy to communicate, and it would be nice if it was as easy as a human getting a dog's message on the big screen.

Grr-eat Solutions Here's a quick communication guide to Dogese 101:

- Howl ("hoowll"). A common cry I use when I'm announcing my spot to a missing pack member (you). I often use this if I'm left home alone.

- Growl ("grrr"). A low internal rumble that is my warning to back off. It's my territory and I'm going to defend it.

- Bark ("woof"). A sound I used during play, greeting, or defense.

- Pant ("heh, heh"). A sound I use if hot, tired, happy, or even in pain.

- Yelp ("yelp"). A dog cry if I'm stepped on or hit that shows I'm in pain.

- Whine ("oomph"). A sound to show I'm in pain but also a good way to get your attention to feed me, let me indoors or outdoors, or to let you know we have visitors.

Pet Peeve #142
Unable to Read My Mind

Despite our good intentions when we do the Lassie whine, humans sometimes don't get it in real life. If we need to tell you something of doggy importance, it is frustrating if you just can't get the telepathic message. If a dog has a new human, it may be impossible for a clear reading of our mind. This is super frustrating to us.

Grr-eat Solution Hook up with a pet psychic. Internet sites offer online pet psychic services. Search under "pet psychics." Here are five tips, with the guidance of animal communicator Mary Getten, who lives on Orcas Island in the San Juan Islands of Washington State, to help you find the best pet psychic for dogs with thoughts on their mind:

- Use a communicator whom someone has recommended. Check pioneer animal communications specialist Penelope Smith's list at www.animaltalk.com. The list will tell you about communicators and some specialties.

- Choose a pet psychic who specializes in what I need (that is, behavioral problems) and has my best interests at heart.

- Ask yourself if the communicator is interested in my problem or more interested in setting up an appointment and getting you off the phone.

- A reputable pet psychic is likely to tell you things about you and your pet that ring uncannily true.

- Use your gut instinct. If something doesn't feel right, contact another communicator.

Canine Tip To understand how dogs can read their humans, fetch the book *Dogs That Know When Their Owners Are Coming Home* by Rupert Sheldrake (Crown Publishers, 2000).

Pet Peeve #143
No Dog Toys

As an alert and active Brittany, if I don't have doggy stuff to stimulate my mind and exercise my body, I will go bonkers. In dog language that means I will rebel and either play with your stuff (such as chew up the sofa or shoes) or amuse myself like the Siberian husky escape artist across the street. He is tied up all day long without toys. And twice a week (out of frustration and spite) he breaks free and the neighborhood becomes his playground.

Grr-eat Solution My point is simple: We dogs need toys. From puppyhood to adult dogdom, we've just got to have bones, balls, educational toys, and more. We are thinkers and doers and it's natural for us to want to busy ourselves like our wild dog ancestors did in the good old days. You can go to pet stores such as PETsMART and Petco to fetch dog toys for our amusement.

Pet Peeve #144
The Wrong Dog Toy

Okay, you get it. Dogs need toys with a capital T. But the glitch is, you've got to get a handle on our personality type so you can get us the right stuff. For instance, I am a bone dog. When my human first brought me home, she was clueless to my bone fetish. So one day I brought out one of her stuffed animals, and another, and another. By the end of the week she had a collection of tattered cats, dogs, and birds. (But I had a stash of new rawhide bones.)

Grr-eat Solution To get a clue about what your dog really wants, observe your pooch. Or read up on our breeds. Here is a quick guide to dog personalities to help you get an idea of what dogs really want:

- Physical Dog. Interactive toys that lure us to retrieve, jump and run with you, such as balls, and Frisbees, are good selections.

- Mental Mutt. Educational things that make us use our canine smarts, such as balls we have to roll to get the kibble from inside, will do the trick.

- Self-Reliant Pup. Toys that amuse us, such as bones we can chew on for hours (without humans), will suffice.

- Spoiled Tyke. We love to be catered to. Think toys that talk and perform for us rather than have us work like a dog to play.

- Couch Pooch. Forget interactive stuff—we're into television. Perhaps a dog video or DVD player so we can watch movies (preferably ones with active dogs) with or without you.

Pet Peeve #145
Not Replacing My Stuff

Once you get us the toy of our dog dreams, it's key that you keep tabs on it. If I can't find my favorite bone, for instance, I will have a catfit. Then I will jump up on the love seat and give my human that bored dog look. Ever notice how sad we look when we don't have our bone or ball? I've got the look down so well that my human will jump up and fetch me a new one ASAP.

Grr-eat Solution If you purchase our favorite dog toys in quantity, we won't have to whine or look lonely and depressed. Also, if you keep on top of our dog toy stash (I think a doggy toy box is a good idea), then we won't annoy you at an inopportune time. The bottom line: You know that we know that our dog toys are a big part of a dog's life. So why would you ever want us to go through withdrawal? Case closed.

Pet Peeve #146
No Playmate

Ah, having dog toys available is bliss, but not having a human to enjoy them with is awful. When you tell us to "fetch your bone" and we eagerly bring it back to you, for example, if there is no praise, it's not fun. We need it acknowledged that we have a toy and you know that we know that we do. Hello—I am a dog. I need to have enthusiastic playmates or you will find me howling.

Grr-eat Solution Personally, as a people-loving Brittany, I like it when my human teams up with me and we play. Also, dogs such as Border collies and Labrador retrievers (there is a photo in our bedroom of my human's former Lab, Carmella, with a Frisbee in her mouth) just love it when they can find a human to toss the flying saucer so they can retrieve it. For me, I love it when I'm told, "Go find your bonie." It makes me feel like I'm a dog who has a purpose in life.

Pet Peeve #147
No Kindergarten

If we don't get to play with other pups and learn basic dog commands, we will be left behind. Translation: We will be a slow dog and socially inept. When we grow up, people will think, *That dog is a canine social outcast.* Worse, we will be ill mannered, unmanageable, and hear "bad dog!" words one too many times, affecting our self-esteem.

Grr-eat Solution Pups need to play with other pups. Obedience classes—puppy-level classes usually called kindergarten classes—provide socialization and basic training for young dogs. We learn obedience commands such as "down" and "stay," and boost our canine abilities to grow up to be well-behaved pooches. And it's never to late to get obedience training or to take a refresher course.

Pet Peeve #148
Vetoed Basic Obedience Classes

It gets on our nerves to hear our humans bark "bad dog!"—especially if they never took us to obedience classes. Chances are, if we get to go to a place that teaches people to communicate with their dogs, we'd be hearing "good dog!" a lot more often. My human didn't take me to obedience classes. Bad human! People often say to us "Dylan has you wrapped around his paw." I am self-taught.

Grr-eat Solution While six months and older is a good age for you to take us to basic obedience classes, it's never too late to teach a human new dog tricks. Translation: Sign us up for obedience classes. Personally, I already know the basic dog commands such as "sit" and "stay," but my human could learn how to heel.

Canine Tip The total cost can be $75 to $105 for a course of six to seven one-hour classes. One-on-one dog trainers charge more than a class. Contact your local humane society for more information on budget group classes.

Pet Peeve #149
No Dog Parenting Training

Ill-educated dogs are products of unhappy dog moms and dads. And it upsets me, a happy Brittany, when I see humans with un-happy dogs. The canine–human bond can be healthful for dogs and humans, but it needs to be nurtured just like parenting a child. If dog people don't treat their dogs like fur children (at whatever age), it will take a toll on our patience. That means we may act out and dig holes or howl songs to show our unhappy feelings.

Grr-eat Solution Happy moms share their dog stories with other happy moms. If they have to work out of the house, they make sure that we are taken care of (for example, doggy day care or dog-friendly workplaces). They know that sharing their life with a four-legger takes time, energy, and money. This, in turn, will allow them to fulfill their need to grasp the rewards of being proud par-ents.

Pet Peeve #150
Being Scolded

"Bad dog!" reprimands can send us away with our tail down and a chip on our doggy shoulder. As a senior dog I can tell you that I don't get "bad dog" scoldings anymore. Years ago, the neighbors thought my name was "No Dylan!" I'm very sensitive, and like other dogs, I can't deal with human emotional outbursts, which can spawn doggy nightmares and bad dog day afternoons.

Being scolded drives dogs up the wall, says Dial-A-Vet Sheree Stern, D.V.M., of Los Angeles, California. "Dogs want to please. That's their goal." In other words, when sensitive dogs, like me, are yelled at, it can make us quiver, and our tail goes down in a flash. My previous human was too stern. I used to curl up in a ball when he would give me harsh scoldings. I hated it.

Grr-eat Solution "One good way to deal with inappropriate behaviors is to provide an alternative acceptable behavior that the dog can choose to engage in," explains Dr. Mary Burch, director of the American Kennel Club's Canine Good Citizen Program. For instance, when we are shredding your favorite shoe, instead of chewing us out for chewing, just take the shoe away and substitute a rawhide bone. Save the temper tantrums for the cat.

Pet Peeve #151
Anti–Pet Shrink

If we are victims of bad words that we'd really rather not hear, expect therapy. Dog therapy, that is. Again, we are sensitive souls. It's irritating that humans can run to the shrink if their love life crumbles—but what about the dog? If we are subjected to "drop it!" "out!" "go away!" and "stop it!" 365 days a year, it's a miracle that we can still function as even-tempered companion animals. And, really, why should we want to?

Grr-eat Solution If our bad dog behavior doesn't get any better, take note. Mr. or Ms. Dog is out of balance. There are telltale hints: no desire to eat with you, living in the closet, or putting in a change of address. If these things are occurring in your household, run, don't walk to your pet shrink.

Canine Tip Contact the American Veterinary Society of Animal Behaviorists (AVSAB) for referrals to certified animal behaviorists through their website at www.avma.org/avsab. Or call Animal Behavior Consultations at (913) 362-2512.

Pet Peeve #152
Dumping Me at the Pound

Bad dog behavioral problems are a big reason why there are throw-away dogs in this world. It's not fair. We are devout people-pleasers and will do almost anything to get praise and do it right (whatever right is). But if you do not allow us to be social and go to doggy school, we will be at the mercy of bad human behavior. Translation: We are taken to the local pound. And yes, it does hurt us a lot to be dumped.

Grr-eat Solution Before you take us away, think. Perhaps we are just incompatible. It happens. A dog may be too active and his human may be too sedentary for them to be happy together. Before you make a rash decision, check out other resources such as placing an ad in the newspaper or contacting a dog rescue group that specializes in finding dogs foster homes.

Canine Tip Dog behavioral problems that are not solved by their humans can and do become a deadly dog problem. More than 56 percent of dogs and puppies entering shelters are euthanized, based on reports from over 1,055 facilities across the United States, according to the National Council on Pet Overpopulation Study and Policy, *Shelter Statistics Survey* (1997 data).

Pet Peeve #153
Uptight Humans

Show dogs (canines who are exhibited for obedience, conformation, and so on.) will agree that the intense vibes of their humans and handlers can be nerve-racking. Show dogs end up believing that dog shows are places where the leader of their pack gets all upset, explains Dr. Stanley Coren. He believes show dogs can sense that every time they go into that familiar building, their human or handler gets all bent out of shape. No doubt, my fellow canines can smell their people sweating, getting upset, and talking in frantic voices to other competitors. In other words, dog shows can bring on a case of walking on eggshells for show dogs.

Grr-eat Solution Chill out! If we don't score, it's not the end of the world. "If you can't relax when you go to a dog show," says Dr. Coren, "have somebody else show your dog. And you walk over into the distance and watch."

Canine Tip Meanwhile, stop and hug the dogs. It's a known fact that interaction with dogs can help lower your blood pressure and reduce stress. (It'll help keep show dogs' blood pressure from soaring, too.)

Pet Peeve #154
Fussing Too Much

Thank goodness I'm not a show dog. I've watched dog shows on Animal Planet, and those handsome pooches must suffer from performance anxiety. Their competitive humans and handlers brush, poke, and place them in position, again and again. Personally, I don't even like to be brushed once a week! All the fidgeting and skittish human behavior may bring on a Shaky Puppy episode for me and perhaps for other sensitive canines, too.

Grr-eat Solution No doubt, it is an ego-boost to compete and win. As a Type A Brittany (driven, competitive, and impatient), I can see the point. It would be a thrill to point in front of an audience! However, the following tension-taming pointers may lessen the fussing and ease the high anxiety:

- Be your dog's best friend before you become a pushy human with prize ribbons on the brain.

- See dog competing as sharing fun rather than expecting canine excellence.

- Practice deep breathing, which will make sensitive canines feel more at ease.

- Seize the moment of show dog joy and play down the pressure of winning.

Canine Tip To pick a good handler, write to the Dog Handler's Guild at 413 Dempsey Avenue Southwest, Buffalo, MN 55313 or call (763) 682-3366.

Pet Peeve #155
Ignoring Me

Performance anxiety or ignoring us—it's like choosing between two evils at dog shows. I have heard my human talk about past dog shows where the prized pups would be exhibited and then *bam*—plopped into crates for hours at a time. How cruel is that? I would feel so used and abused.

Grr-eat Solution I beg all handlers and humans involved in showing their talented dogs to be attentive to their four-leggers before, during, and after their canine performance. Be sure our mind, body, and spirit is nourished (whether we win or lose). Our tail wags and dog smiles depend on it.

Pet Peeve #156
Anti-Dog Lodging

Why can't dog lovers pamper their prized pups (show dogs or not) like the rich and famous? Reality bites when you have to sneak me into fancy hotels because of a big NO DOGS ALLOWED sign on the premises. I don't understand why you can't find out where pooches are pampered, then get the leash and take me on vacation with you. I wouldn't think of going to a bed-and-breakfast without you.

Grr-eat Solution Make it a positive experience (for both of us) and we'll have a great place to come back to. Don't leave us unattended in a hotel room unless you can arrange for a dog-friendly petsitter while you're gone. Damage done by other dogs makes us unwelcome. Pet-friendly lodging varies from simple to luxurious accommodations. A pet fee may be charged and varies with the facility. Some hotels may require a deposit or credit card in the event of doggy damage.

Canine Tip Many Holiday Inns are dog-friendly. Sniff out their website at www.6C.com and go to the link Plan Your Route, or call (800) 465-4329. Also, check out the websites www.petsonthego.com, which provides travel tips and dog-friendly lodging, and www.dogfriendly.com, a travel guide for dogs that includes hotels and much more.

6. Heart and Soul Barks

Pet Peeve #157
Too Much Action

If there is too much going on, we may indulge in "bad dog" activity. (Read: bark, snap, and such.) Either way, sometimes too much action (such as when we're at an extravagant pooch party) exasperates us. I can personally attest to this. For instance, I enjoyed a garden party a few years back. However, after running free with other dogs (keep in mind, I'm an active Brittany), Anna, a strong-willed rottweiler, snapped at me. She wanted to lie down and regroup. I got the message.

Grr-eat Solution Getting dog tired after too much action is not unusual for dogs. It's normal for dogs, like Anna, to crave a "safe spot" to go to. This can be under a chair or tree. At home, if there are too many guests some of us will sniff out a bedroom closet or quiet room. In fact, it couldn't hurt for a human to play guide person to an overwhelmed canine during hectic social events and lead us to a quiet refuge.

Pet Peeve #158
Not Enough Action

On the flip side, if I, the sensitive Bird Dog, am all by myself, I am going to be howling the blues. Why? I am a social animal. Think the "Original Bud Light Party Animal" Spuds Mackenzie. Like this bull terrier, I am a human magnet. I can't cope if I am left alone too long or if I don't have a chance to socialize with people or dogs. Worse, if you keep dogs, like me, sheltered and then one day toss us into an intense social situation, it will be a shock, especially if you've kept us on a short leash.

Grr-eat Solution   Take us to the dog park on a regular basis. Going for a walk in a park where dogs are allowed offers a natural way to socialize. We will get our fix of dog and people action and therefore will not cringe or freak out when you decide to come out of your shell and socialize.

Canine Tip   Contact your local park and recreation center to find dog parks and learn about the regulations (such as leash requirements) in your area.

Pet Peeve #159
Boring Humans

Most dogs, like me, are compatible with people who have a sense of humor. Imagine: As a natural-born bird flusher, I attempt to catch a housefly and land smack on my face in the living room. I am uninhibited. I am Dog. And if you can't chuckle at my impromptu amusing antics, it's disturbing, because dogs are comedians who appreciate an appreciative audience.

Grr-eat Solution Humans need to lighten up and join in the fun with their canine clown. Whether we are clever or klutzy, it's time to home in to our type of sense of humor and enjoy it. Next time you are in a no-nonsense mood, take a break. Let the dog in you come out and play. If not, please have an on-call pet pal for us to visit at the times you're not in the mood to have fun.

Canine Tip According to the 2001 AAHA Pet Owner Survey, 59 percent of the 1,210 respondents reported that their pet has a best pet friend.

Pet Peeve #160
Not Waking Me Up

Serious humans will let dogs sleep through serious dog things. It bugs me when my human takes advantage of important canine events. Hey, what if a squirrel or burglar is on our property and I'm snoring? If you let me, the protector of the household, get too relaxed, it will make me feel useless or like I just missed the boat.

Grr-eat Solution If something of dog importance happens, gently wake me up and say, "Puppy, wake up. We need you now." Not only does this make us feel like VIPs (very important pooches), but we can be your loyal protector and do our job. If you promise to wake us up, we promise to stop barking upon command (unless it's the postman).

Pet Peeve #161
No Baby Talk

During my waking hours, I confess that as a gentle Brittany I wouldn't feel complete without sweet human words. The neighbor's dog never gets baby talk. One day when my human and I were outside she asked me, "Are you having fun in the snow, Puppy Pie?" Meanwhile, we both heard, "Get in here you stupid mutt!" (he's a purebred!) bellowed across the street. My tail dropped down for the old dog—a two-year-old pooch.

Grr-eat Solution We dogs love to hear nice words from our mom and dad in a nice tone. It makes us feel good all over. Remember, we are sensitive, and baby talk is a wonderful way to enhance the canine–human bond. Wait, I hear my human calling now: "Where oh where is my angel dog? Mommy loves you." Ah, my heart is melting.

Canine Tip According to the 2001 AAHA Pet Owner Survey, forty-eight percent of the 1,211 respondents reported that they say "I love you" to their pet more than once daily.

Pet Peeve #162
Not Sharing Meals

We don't get it when humans hoard their food and don't give us our cut. It's not fair. One day, like always, I watched my human make lunch. As a pack animal, I anticipated getting in on the find. But she hoarded "our" food. My doggy stare didn't work. All I got was a "No Dylan. It's mine." How selfish is that? Dogs are used to hunting for food and sharing our find.

Grr-eat Solution Be consistent. If you don't want us to beg, then be firm and don't send us mixed signals: One day we score; the next day we don't. We are dogs and don't understand why people can be generous and then stingy. Keep the rules simple and we can play the game.

Canine Tip If you can't take your dog to Europe, a place where dogs are allowed in many restaurants, hit the dog bakeries in America. Go online and type in "dog bakeries," then grab a pencil and the dog leash.

Pet Peeve #163
Off Limits to Postman

While dogs love to eat, some of us, like me, live to bark at the postman. "This is an intruder who is definitely trying to do harm to me or you. The proof of the matter is, he's sticking stuff through that slot and desperately trying to hit us," explains Dr. Stanley Coren. "The dogs know that, in fact, their attack on your mail (and the noise which they made) made him go away. They know that every day he's going to come in and attack. They're going to defend the pack," he adds. And it bugs me, an alert dog, when I am told to "stop it."

Grr-eat Solution "The first thing to do is to cover the mailbox. Hang a basket over the mailbox so the dog can't shred your mail," suggests Dr. Coren. I recommend that you go to his plan B: Put me in my pet room and turn up the tunes. (My choice, please.) But note, if you live in one room, save your money and invest in a post office box. This way we won't have to play the Protect My Human From the Postal Worker game anymore and you won't go "postal."

Pet Peeve #164
Putting Your Work First

Working like a dog and ignoring your dog is for the birds. It aggravates us when our humans work overtime, do double shifts, or take on two jobs. Sure, the bills need to be paid, but hey, what about me? Dogs cannot live on work alone. It dulls the mind and body.

Grr-eat Solution You've got two choices: Get us a job or take us with you to work. We're easy. The point is, please don't ignore us and pretend we'll go away. We need to keep busy like you or we'll go bonkers and resort to barking and digging to pass the time.

Canine Tip Dog actors can make big bucks but it takes a while to hit it big. (In other words, don't quit your day job.)

Pet Peeve #165
Hating My Dog Friends

We are social critters. It bugs us when you label our canine chums "a cat chaser" or "a mutt" and try and keep us from hanging out together. Just because a pet pal chases cats doesn't mean that we will. And isn't it a tad snippy to forbid purebreds to play with mongrels? I don't get it. Dogs are dogs. Let us play for dog's sake.

Grr-eat Solution Doggy day care is like day care for kids. While our humans do their thing, we can socialize with different dogs in a supervised facility. Day care centers provide housetraining and obedience training, which usually includes basic commands and doggy manners. I can have a broad circle of dog friends in a safe environment and you won't have to worry about unwanted consequences.

Canine Tip Check out the Yellow Pages for doggy day care facilities in your area. Fees range from $8 to $25 or more daily. We must have a current health certificate from our vets, and dogs older than eight months of age must be spayed or neutered.

Pet Peeve #166
Anti–Mixed Breeds

This peeve is part two of Pet Peeve #165. Actually, I am registered with the American Kennel Club, but I am not partial to purebreds. I am open-minded and like all dogs. Did you know that there are purebred dog people and breedists? Yep, there are people out there who favor purebreds or one breed in particular. I don't like restrictions. It bugs me because I like to play with all dog breeds. However, I do prefer the female gender.

Grr-eat Solution Personally, it doesn't bother me if a dog is a mutt or purebred. I've had fun with both. Both kinds of females were fun-loving and I couldn't tell the difference. Plenty of people believe that mixed breeds are friendlier and smarter than purebreds. Remember Higgens in *Benji the Hunted?* The scruffy cream-colored terrier mix boasted both smarts and compassion toward other animals. Since the shelters are full of unwanted mixed breeds, it's time more people get smart and become pro-mutt. Mixed breeds generally cost less—or are free.

Canine Tip The Mixed Breed Dog Clubs of America will give you information on mixed breeds. Call (740) 259-3941, or go to its website at www.mbdca.org.

Pet Peeve #167
Human Arguments

Worse than anti-mixed-breed humans are humans who can't get along. It can wreak havoc on our fragile canine nerves. We loathe it when Mom and Dad argue. We can't handle it when a couple start yelling and calling each other names. It scares us. We think, *Is it my fault?* Often, we'll look guilty, cower, and flee to seek refuge.

Grr-eat Solution You can keep us calm by making our household as stress-free as possible. Try to resolve relationship issues away from me. "If you simply must have the shootout at the OK Corral with your partner or children, it may be a good time for your dog to take a break in the yard or go into a crate," says pet shrink Dr. Mary Burch. And if you find me, your beloved canine in the closet, it's time to make some changes.

Canine Tip Your local humane society will be able to refer you to an animal behaviorist to help me with problems related to your stress.

Pet Peeve #168
Divorce—Who Gets the Dog?

If you're divorced (or soon to be), sensitive pooches, like me, can sense it. When two people avoid one another, we can sense this, too. As social pack animals, it disrupts our well-being when our family is out of sorts. It makes us so unbalanced that we will turn to hiding in the closet or living under the bed. We may turn to attention-getters such as chewing on your shoes or couch. Or some dogs may run away from home in the hope of finding a calmer place.

Grr-eat Solution   Take us to therapy if divorce is in the cards. Dogs can't deal with this. We all need counseling when a divorce takes place. It wreaks havoc on both human and canine nerves. (See Pet Peeve #167.) "In the case of separation, remember that your dog is an innocent victim. Ideally, both parties will work to make sure the dog is given the placement that is in the dog's best interest," says Dr. Burch. Also, to avoid a messy divorce settlement, get down in writing whose dog I am and where you want me to go after a divorce.

Canine Tip   To find an attorney who specializes in animal law in your state, contact In Defense of Animals at (415) 388-9641 or go to its website at www.idausa.org.

Pet Peeve #169
Spooky Stuff

What's worse than Mom and Dad getting a divorce? A quake, hurricane, tornado, or fire. According to scientists, dogs' super senses make us more sensitive to the Earth's changes so we can get spooked before you do. When the magnetic field fluctuates a few days, hours, minutes, or even seconds before a tremor, when there are changes in the weather, or when smoke fills the air, we can feel disoriented or scared. Since I am a California native, I am used to having the ground shake violently. And as a Shaky Pup, you would think I could handle tremors. Not so.

Grr-eat Solution Next time we start acting strangely, consider heading for safer ground. Better yet, have a box with our dog name on it by the door. In this we want our dog leash, food (the good stuff, please), and blanket. (Bones are a must-have.) Please note that our success rate in predicting quakes isn't perfect. There are many other things that can trigger our reactions, such as the visiting dog next door or an unhappy feral cat. Perhaps monitoring both the cat and dog for unusual behavior is a good idea if you want to be earthquake-ready.

Canine Tip Keep up to date on other pets' predictions of earthquakes. Check out the Earthquake Prediction newsletter (available at $40 per year) on the website at www.syzygyjob.net. The editor is Jim Berkland, and the address is Box 1926, Glen Ellen, CA 95442.

Pet Peeve #170
Thunder and Lightning

As a Shaky Pup, I don't like quakes and I don't like loud noises. Thunderbolts and lightning strikes freak me out. I may bolt under the bed. It's my wild dog survival instinct. It's worse when my human acts scared, too. Like, who is going to protect us? This isn't the pizza guy (I can take care of him)—it's Mother Nature paying a social call.

Grr-eat Solution According to Dr. Burch, it's best not to "feed into the fear" by pampering me and saying, "There, there Pooch." This is the time for you to protect me (hey, I've been protecting you for a long time). "The key thing is for you to act like everything is under control," she says. So turn on the tunes or tune us into Animal Planet's *The Planet's Funniest Animals* program and let's pretend everything is cool.

Pet Peeve #171
Natural Disaster Unpreparedness

Fires, floods, and other disasters can and do happen. Dogs can't do anything to plan ahead, but their humans can prepare. Last night I was watching television with my human. She said, "Look, Dylan. See the doggy swim for his life." I watched my fellow canine fight the raging floodwaters and then climb up on top of a house rooftop and wait desperately for a rescue team. ("Hoowll.") Later on, I had a doggy bad dream. It was a rude wake-up call that my human, like other dog people, isn't prepared for the Big One.

Grr-eat Solution See Pet Peeve #72 and follow the tips straight from The Humane Society of the United States. If it works for the cat, it's good enough for me. Meanwhile, it couldn't hurt to get an extra big bag (or two) of bones for safety's sake. We don't want to be without. That would be another disaster.

Pet Peeve #172
No Birthday Party

Birthday celebrations are for humans only, right? Wrong. If you think that pooch parties are unconventional, think again. It irritates me that some humans think it's dumb to celebrate a dog's birthday. After all, dogs are party animals. And the fact remains, as social creatures we may even get the birthday blues if you never let us get wild and crazy with humans and fellow canines. Plus, I have American Kennel Club (AKC) papers that prove that I was born on September 22. So there is no excuse for my human to forget my birthday.

Grr-eat Solution Plan us a birthday party just like you would for a human, but with a doggy touch. Go ahead—pick a theme; send out invitations; decorate the house; create a menu plan; plan doggy games and activities; buy favors, prizes, doggy treats, and a canine cake; and don't forget cleanup. (Disposable plates, doggy bowls, and pooper scoopers are required.) ("Woof.")

If you do it yourself, you'll save money and appreciate the outcome because it will be just the way you and your dog want it. Dog party helpers include companies such as Three Dog Bakery, which has frozen canine cakes like peanut butter and carob chip to choose from. Each cake serves up to eight dogs and can be delivered in twenty-four to forty-eight hours.

Here's a convenient guide for dog party resources (for a variety of holidays) to get you on the ball:

- Doggy-Do and Pussycats, Too!, 567 Third Avenue, New York, NY 10016; (212) 661-0111; www.doggydo.com
- Pet Celebrations, 269 North Highland Avenue, Elmhurst, IL 60126; (877) 860-8380; www.petcelebrations.com
- Three Dog Bakery, 1627 Main Street, Suite. 700, Kansas City, MO 64108; www.threedog.com

Canine Tip Check out pet horoscopes online to try to figure out your dog's birth month if you don't know it.

Pet Peeve #173
Fourth of July

While celebrating my birthday is great, count me out on Independence Day. Call me the sensitive Bird Dog, but to be honest with you, firecrackers and sparklers don't make my tail wag. The unexpected pop and sizzle of fireworks turn me into a scaredy-cat. In fact, you can find me under the bed with the cat. I like the socialization part, but lose the noise or I am doggone.

Grr-eat Solution The Fourth of July is high-anxiety time for pets, cautions Ted Cohn, D.V.M., with the AAHA. He recommends the following:

- Keep me away from all fireworks. (See! I was right.) Burns, hearing loss, and eye damage can happen if I am too close for comfort.

- Dump all the remaining fireworks. I don't want to be tempted to eat leftover fragments, which can cause digestive woes or serious injuries.

- Be sure I'm wearing a pet identification tag. If I'm super nervous and frightened, I may try to flee.

Pet Peeve #174
Halloween

When October 31 rolls around, dogs, like me, either flee or bark nonstop at each and every knock on the door. Worse, visitors wearing skeleton costumes and scarecrow outfits don't help my canine patrol. I have to be on guard way too long. If I start shaking in my paws or growling, don't be surprised. This holiday is no dog party.

Grr-eat Solution Let's break tradition and play doggone. Turn out the lights, shut the blinds, and let's play couch potato in the bedroom. We can cuddle and have our own celebration. Bring some doggy treats. If you must, grab the cat and let's tune in to a romantic Lifetime movie for cheap thrills.

Canine Tip Beware of pet pranksters year-round. Check out The American Society for the Prevention of Cruelty to Animals at www.aspca.org.

Pet Peeve #175
Thanksgiving

Just when I get through Halloween, another holiday hits. It's frustrating to watch that bird be cooked all day and then be told, "Dogs can't have table scraps." According to Dr. Jan Strother, an AAHA vet from Hartsville, Alabama, "Most dogs will not chew the bone thoroughly, and sharp pieces can cause blockage and perforate the intestinal tract." I hate Thanksgiving. So what's a Bird Dog to do?

Grr-eat Solution Plan ahead. So I won't sneak turkey from the table, order doggy treats or make me something special. By watching you hustle and bustle in the kitchen and then reward me with goodies, I won't miss that big bird—well, not much anyway. But hey, to make me feel part of the family, you can purchase a bag of biscuit mix with a bone-shaped cookie cutter at specialty pet shops.

Canine Tip If I sneak turkey from the table, be on the alert, says Dr. Strother, because bones in a dog's tummy may not cause any symptoms for twenty-four to forty-eight hours. Warning: If we don't eat, are depressed, or act sick to our stomach, call the vet ASAP.

Pet Peeve #176
Christmas

While the Thanksgiving bird can disrupt my well-being, Christmas has its own set of problems for dogs. The way I see it, decorated trees and lights are booby traps for klutzy dogs, like me. Holiday plants, ornaments, pine needles, and sweets are like mines to a dog. How do I know what's dog-safe and what's not?

Grr-eat Solution According to the AAHA, there are six common holiday hazards that can wreak havoc on a dog's body, like mine. Please take note of my personal comments:

- Christmas tree. If your tree isn't well secured it can come tumbling down and scare the daylights out of me! And note, if that water at the base has tree-saving chemicals in it, you may end up rescuing me if I take a drink.

- Electrical cords. Those holiday lights equal electrical cords for me to chew or get tangled up in. Not fun.

- Holiday plants. Mistletoe is not dog-friendly. If it's in my reach and I nibble on it, you can nix doggy kisses.

- Ornaments. Speaking of non–dog edibles: Yarns, ribbons, and tinsel can mean a trip to the pet E.R. if I get into it and can't get it out of my throat or tummy.

- Pine needles. And if I gobble up pine needles you can kiss my doggy intestines good-bye.

- Sweets. Ignore my begging for chocolate. It contains a pet-deadly caffeinelike chemical called theobromine that can shorten my life lickety-split.

Pet Peeve #177
New Feline Roomie

Just when everything in a dog's world is calm, our humans bring home a new cat. We dogs mull, *Am I not enough pet for you?* or *Did I do something wrong?* We don't understand. For example, when that black-and-white cat entered our household, I was curious. It's not like I haven't lived with cats before. I'm indifferent. But the cat didn't know that. Thank goodness, he was more confused than me.

Grr-eat Solution "If cats and dogs come together at older ages in the family, until you are absolutely sure the relationship will be a good one, you should provide supervision during all interactions," says Dr. Burch. And my human did just that. On Day Two (the first day Kerouac hung out in the study) she let him observe me, the gentleman dog, for a while. He sized me up, and within twenty-four hours he let me know that he was Top Cat and we have gotten along fine ever since. Um, I think I hear Kerouac meowing now. I have to go and see what he needs.

Pet Peeve #178
New Pup

A new adult cat, like Kerouac, is fine. But a frisky puppy for a senior dog, like me? I think I'll pass. Perhaps if the other dog was a female (a fun-loving Brittany named Bambi), I would consider it. But I may feel upstaged. Here's a cautionary tale I overhead one day from my human: When her black Labrador retriever was introduced to her family's new addition, Carmella, a yellow eight-week-old Lab, his life changed. The bubbly pup's overbearing personality overwhelmed him. He took up residence in the bedroom closet. I cringe when I hear that story. Poor old Stonefox.

Grr-eat Solution Think twice about adopting a second dog, especially if you have a senior canine, like me. True, another pooch could liven up a dog's life. But on the other hand, I am currently the solo Puppy Pie, and I don't know if I really want to give up my alpha dog position. (I already let Kerouac, Mr. Cat, boss me around. Enough is enough.)

Pet Peeve #179
Playing Favorites

While we're on the subject of new pets, it's important to dogs that we are not taken for granted or ignored. As pack animals, we will work out the order in the dog family without your help. However, if you begin to play favorites, such as walking one of us more than the other, you'll be stepping over the dog–human line. Indeed, dogs have feelings, and you will be properly notified. (Remember Stoney's actions? Dogs who retreat to closets are sending a strong telepathic message.)

Grr-eat Solution If you decide to bring home another cat or dog, play fair. Schedule quality time for all the companion animals. Spread your love, time, and patience around and make it a family affair like an animal spin-off of *The Waltons*. Forget about spoiling one animal and ignoring the other. It will keep our tail wagging and you won't have to witness a sad and forgotten closet dog. Poor Stonefox.

Pet Peeve #180
Anti-Dog Mate

Finding the ideal canine guardian is not easy. So I can imagine how hard it is to find a dog-loving significant other. (My dog-loving human is still single and looking.) I, for one, would not be a happy camper if my human brought home a person who treats dogs like dogs. If you're romancing a potential mate who doesn't treat dogs like they are part of the family, I say move on. It will never work out.

Grr-eat Solution To meet a genuine dog lover, you've got to hang out where the dogs do. Hit the dog parks and dog bakeries. Or place an ad in the personals. Be creative and write something like "Tired of conversations with Fido. Seek human dog lover." And note, if you want to be with dog lovers, don't flock with anti-dog people. Get serious. Think of serious dog people who love and write about dogs such as Jack London and John Steinbeck. It's these type of people who are suitable for my mistress and me.

Canine Tip According to the 2001 AAHA Pet Owner Survey, 90 percent of the 1,152 respondents said they would not consider dating someone who wasn't fond of their pet.

Pet Peeve #181
Bully Dogs

If dogs won't settle for bully people, we certainly won't adapt to a bully dog. Read: We won't tolerate an inconsiderate self-serving canine. It doesn't matter what size a dog is, it's more about tempera ment. Bullies can include unpredictable dogs who are too aggressive, canines thieves who steal other dogs' toys, and possessive pooches who overprotect their humans. A bully, who can be of any breed or age, can make or break a well-mannered dog's day. For me, a protective Brittany, I think I can whip any bully dog. But my human insists that a German shepherd or Great Dane could make dogmeat out of me. What does that mean?

Grr-eat Solution It does help if your human can size up the dog and determine what to do. For example, if you're at a dog park or walking in the neighborhood, there are ways to avoid dogfights. "Out in a park area, you really need to keep your dogs on leashes," points out Dr. Wayne Hunthausen. Also, if we get nervous around dogs whom we don't know, let their humans know it. If a stray dog is on the loose, plan an escape route and I'll follow you.

Pet Peeve #182
Unsavory Strangers

Bully dogs, bully people—they're the same to me. Personally, I can sense bad vibes in a fearful human, or canine, which can make me react like a dog. ("Grrr.") If someone behaves scared in my presence, my first thought will be *You're hiding something*. Dogs have heightened senses and can feel when someone is suspicious or a threat to our well-being. It puts us on high alert. We are ready to defend you or our territory.

Grr-eat Solution More times than not, when we sense a bad animal or bad person we'll be right on the money. My best advice is to trust us and then let the chips fall where they may. Sometimes, it may take a while for us to accept a new person, but if that is the case there may be a good reason behind it. In other words, proceed with caution if our growling persists.

Pet Peeve #183
Excluded From Family Fun

I feel so sad when I'm left out of family activities, whether they involve running errands or going to the beach. It's all relative. When you go anywhere without me I go into my "Woe Is Me" dog mode. Worse, separation anxiety sets in. Says Dr. Burch, "Sometimes dogs seem to be sullen when they are not involved in activities and the owner is home. These are dogs who perceive the family as a pack and as a pack member, the dog would like to be involved in family activities."

Grr-eat Solution Dr. Burch adds, "As the owner, you are in charge of the pack in your household. You get to decide which activities your dog can participate in. Remember that dogs are social animals, your dog loves you, and you owe it to this dog to give it quality time and attention."

Canine Tip Start including us in family fun ASAP. "By including your puppy in activities, you're going to get a healthy, happy, well-adjusted, laid-back dog. Dogs that are the friendliest are the dogs that spend lots of time with their people," says Dr. Jeffrey Masson.

Pet Peeve #184
Closing the Car Windows

While we're on the subject of family activities . . . Why do some humans roll up the window if their dog is in a groove, sniffing the fresh air, the wind blowing in our face, ears flapping back? As a sporting dog, I would be upset if my human closed the car window. (I don't care if it is cold or not.) I love to get a whiff of fresh air. I had to train my human (I used heavy sulking corrections) to let me, Dylan, have the shotgun seat in the car. But other dogs aren't as lucky. I see them on the road sulking.

Grr-eat Solution I know that vets have documented reports of dogs who get debris in their eyes by sitting in an open truck bed or hanging their head out the car window. So let's cut a deal: If we're not in an area where road work is being done or a tornado just hit, can I do it?

Canine Tip Check out sporting goods stores for kids' swimming goggles to protect doggy eyes. If you can't find them, perhaps this can be a moneymaking novelty business for you to start.

Pet Peeve #185
Leaving Me Outdoors

While the great outdoors is wonderful, when the winter or summertime hits, the wonder can plummet. As a senior dog, I'm more sensitive to cold. Luckily, I am an indoor dog (I just play outdoors). However, I have seen neighborhood dogs weather both the snow and heat because their humans leave them outdoors day and night. I hear them barking and howling up a storm. The fact is, some dogs (especially if they're young, old, or fragile) can't handle the stress of being outside in freezing temperatures (unless they're northern dogs such as the Alaskan malamute). And summer heat can be oh-so grueling to those of us with a heavy coat.

Grr-eat Solution Make sure we have warm quarters when the winter winds howl. And in the summer months, be aware that we (especially seniors, like me) are more vulnerable to heatstrokes. A cool place to rest and lots of fresh water to drink are advised.

Canine Tip According to the AAHA, parked cars are potential death traps for us during the warm months. Remember, dogs wear fur coats year-round. Don't leave us in a parked car in the winter, either. Some of us, like Chihuahuas, are hairless.

Pet Peeve #186
Dumping Me at the Kennel

I'd rather go to a kennel than be left outdoors. But getting rid of the dog so you can go on vacation is so unfair. Personally, I will suffer from separation anxiety. Strange people, strange dogs, and a strange environment. It's not my idea of dog love to dump me in a 6- by 6-foot dog cell with food and water. Sounds like doggy prison, huh? ("Hoowll.")

Grr-eat Solution If you have to go somewhere without me (and can't find an available petsitter), there are boarding facilities that can make my time alone a doable experience. For instance, the Ritzy Canine Carriage House in New York City is a pet-friendly hotel to die for. The amenities include twenty-four-hour fully attended service, cageless day care, exercise in a parklike setting, and nightly turndown service for all guests. All the comforts of home—perhaps more. For more information, call (212) 949-1818.

Canine Tip To help you find a dog-friendly kennel, write to the American Boarding Kennel Association at 4575 Galley Road, Suite 400 A, Colorado Springs, CO 80915 or visit its website at www.abka. com.

Pet Peeve #187
Letting Me Run Stray

Kennels are confining, but letting me run wild has its pitfalls, too. My human told me about one senior golden retriever in the San Francisco Bay Area. Good-natured Ralph was left on his own, with a bag of dog kibble and a pail of water, to roam the streets as his irresponsible human vacationed in Mexico. I like free runs, but being left on our own, like Ralph, is inhumane. To me, after ten minutes running stray without supervision is like a sci-fi movie. Cars, strangers, coyotes—it's deadly. Worse, if the dog catcher is out, I will be caught and taken to the pound (which is worse than a kennel).

Grr-eat Solution   Humans often blame us for being escape artists and taking to the streets to run wild. To curb our appetite for free runs, may I suggest daily dog walks or runs? It's your job to make sure that the fence in our yard is secure. It's a dog's job to dig our way out like humans do in prison movies. Think what canine diggers can do.

Canine Tip   Pet overpopulation is not helped by letting dogs run stray or neglecting to get a dog neutered or spayed (an operation to prevent reproduction). Contact SPAY/USA at (800) 248-SPAY or log on to www.spayusa.org.

Pet Peeve #188
Not Picking Me at the Pound

Ever see how lonely my fellow dogs look at the dog pound? They are starved for freedom and affection. Yet day after day, homeless canines (purebreds and mutts) pace in their cell waiting for someone to walk by and rescue them. This isn't any way for a dog to live. That irks me a lot.

Grr-eat Solution Dogs at the pound are in need of good homes. Shelters have a policy that the pooches need to be neutered or spayed, have up-to-date vaccinations, and be in good health. Also, humans get to choose from among mixed breeds and purebreds. Most important, my canine senses tell me that homeless dogs are thrilled to be picked and placed in a loving dog-friendly home.

Canine Tip For more information on spaying and neutering, and rescuing unwanted dogs, call the Doris Day Animal Foundation at (202) 546-1761 or log on to www.ddaf.org.

Pet Peeve #189
Being a Latchkey Dog

My neighbors know that I, "that orange-and-white barking dog," detest being home alone. They hear my howls of protest. According to Dr. Coren, sporting dogs such as golden and Labrador retrievers "go absolutely crazy home alone." No wonder I howl up a storm.

"Dogs have busy, bright, active minds and they are social creatures. Left alone at home all day, they can get into trouble," adds Dr. Burch. Read: We self-destruct or destroy our human's stuff. My favorite *Home Alone* activities include incessant howling, barking, and putting my white furry paws deep into the love seat. I peer out the living room window. I have been told that I look like I just lost my best friend.

Grr-eat Solution To help us de-stress before you leave us all alone, it may be beneficial to go for a doggy walk. Make sure you fill our water bowl with fresh H_2O (reread Pet Peeve #107), and please leave us with something creative to do. "Chew toys are good ideas for dogs who get bored," says Dr. Burch. Most likely, they're your best bet because they will help deter us from chewing up your favorite things out of spite. Or may I suggest getting the dog-friendly kid on the block to pay me a visit (or two) and take me for a walk? And I will gladly welcome a professional pet-sitter to keep me company.

Canine Tip For referrals to petsitters in your area, contact Pet Sitters International at www.petsit.com, or the National Association of Professional Pet Sitters at www.petsitters.org.

Pet Peeve #190
Postponing "Let's Go Bye Bye"

This is one of my mega pet peeves. Imagine how excited we dogs get when our humans announce "Let's Go Bye Bye." My problem is, why in the dog world then do you do something else and ignore us? You get our tail up, our four paws ready for action, and then *bam*— it's a no-go. Personally, as a Go Dog, I'm devastated. "It's inconsistent communication," says Dr. Coren. "Dogs have the mind of a two-year-old. Suppose you told a two-year-old, 'We're going to go outside to the park.' And then you pick up the telephone and ignore them for the next twenty minutes." The outcome: A temper tantrum.

Grr-eat Solution Dr. Coren recommends, "Do not say things or prepare to do things which you have no intention of following through." Yep, dog experts know that it's unfair to get me all excited and then let me down. I'm just a dog and I can't handle wishy-washy humans. Either you want to do something now or you don't. Please don't send me mixed signals.

Pet Peeve #191
Lying to Me

Worse than postponing the dog outing is killing it. One winter day my human told me that we were going to go "bye bye." I anticipated the Big Event. I eagerly watched her get dressed, lock up the house, and get her car keys and my dog leash. Then, at the last minute, the words "It's too cold for you Puppy Pie. You won't like waiting in the car" hit hard. I was thinking, *No I won't. Hey, no really, I can deal with it.* Despite my attempt at telepathic communication I was left home alone. I was devastated. This pet peeve is an extension of Pet Peeve #190. All talk, no action. The words "Let's go for a walk" or "Do you want a piece of fresh turkey?" may not happen. You lie to us, man's best friend. It's unacceptable human behavior. We just hate it. ("Grrr.")

Grr-eat Solution The remedy for Pet Peeve #191 is simple, say animal experts. Don't give us a verbal cue such as "Hey Boy, let's go for a run!" or "It's doggy treat time!" unless you're ready to follow through. In other words, if there's any chance it'll be a no-go, keep the announcement to yourself. We sensitive dogs can't handle the bad news. It's a major letdown.

Pet Peeve #192
Stupid Dog Tricks

Why do you demean us in front of your human friends? The last time my human had the gang over, what did she do? She barked the "Shake" command to me with ten eyeballs staring at me, waiting for me to perform. How can people do this to their beloved dog? I felt so threatened. "The reason dogs don't like it is because everybody stares at them. And staring is a threat, especially if people stare and open their mouth and show their teeth," explains Dr. Coren.

Grr-eat Solution   We can compromise. If you want us to perform doggy tricks to amuse you, we will. However, I, for one, prefer to do this on a one-to-one basis. No audience. Translation: It's you and me, babe. This way, you'll get comic relief and I'll preserve my self-worth. P. S. Don't forget the dog treats.

Pet Peeve #193
Dog Ageist Attitude

As a senior dog, this prejudice—which we tag "dog-ageism," discrimination against dogs because they are old (like breedists and specists discriminate against dog breeds and species)—bothers me a lot. Perhaps my coat is not as shiny as it once was. And my cataracts bug me, too. Okay, so I may have a potty accident once or twice. And when I hear my human tap a pencil I run to the door thinking we have a visitor. But hey, I'm twelve and a half years old!

Remember the dog who played the memorable lead role in the film *White Fang*? The wolf-malamute was twelve during the shoot. My human asked Jed's dog trainer, Clint Rowe, how his aging canine superstar remained so active. "A lot of it is just happiness," replied Rowe. "Good diet. Good care."

Grr-eat Solution There are humans who think themselves young by doing what makes their heart sing. Dr. Coren recommends that you do exactly the same for senior pups, like me. Here are some think-young ways to help us accept the aging process:

- Give me my share of one-on-one time.
- Act happy with me.
- Take me back to obedience class. (I don't want to get senile!)
- Expect the best. Dogs live longer these days. (As a Brittany I can live to at least fourteen—that's seventy-five or more in dog years.)
- Don't sweat the small stuff. So what if I get a few aches and pains. I have you to massage my dog body from head to tail.
- Take me to new dog activities to keep me on the ball physically and mentally.

Canine Tip Check out the Senior Dog Project's website at www. srdogs.com. It includes a guide to the conditions of and medications for mature dogs, and offers tips for helping older dogs enjoy life.

Pet Peeve #194
Putting Me Down Too Soon

Despite our age, we can be put to sleep for absurd reasons. It's not fair. But doggy homicide happens every day. Some humans will give us a one-way ticket to doggy heaven if we don't get up and respond to a verbal cue like we used to. This is a lame reason to bid good riddance to Mr. or Ms. Dog. Whatever happened to respect for your canine elders?

Grr-eat Solution If you are seriously mulling over doggy heaven time, it seems fair to seek another opinion (or two) before calling it quits. Consult with a vet and a pet psychic if you really think it's time to say good-bye. Sometimes we may not be ready to leave this planet. In some cases Good Samaritans, such as vets, will see this and be our rescuer.

Pet Peeve #195
Not Putting Me Down

If I'm pondering doggy suicide, however, it's time to wake up and feel my pain. I recall a tale about Hubert, a seventeen-year-old mixed breed who lived longer than he should have. But his humans just couldn't bear to let their loyal canine go. He had to be carried outside to go potty, needed to be spoon-fed, and was bedridden. Poor Hubert. His life was over but he had to linger on like a good old dog. His feelings were not considered.

Grr-eat Solution Again, it's time to bring in a professional animal expert to help you to decide if it's time to say good-bye or not. It's a difficult decision. But if our quality of life is plummeting and we just aren't enjoying life, it may be in our best interest to let us go in peace.

Pet Peeve #196
Not Dealing With It

It's difficult for dogs to let go of their humans. And perhaps, we sense when on the other side that our humans can't move on. That troubles me. My human, for instance, told me the story of when she took her ebony Lab Stonefox with her on a business trip. (He was her loyal travel companion during the freewheeling 1970s, when she hitchhiked across America.) The clincher is, this time, she was traveling with her beloved deceased dog-in-a-box. It was a sentimental journey but . . . it's not my style. Really, it must be heartbreaking to dog angels knowing that their past humans can't get a grip.

Grr-eat Solution One way to get closure is to take out an ad bidding your last good-bye to me, your beloved dog. Pet owners started running pet memorials in the *Philadelphia Daily News.* These pet obituaries run monthly under the heading "A Fond Farewell to Our Beloved Pet." Be concise; use phrases such as "Get the Frisbee!" Not only will you save money with a one-line ad, you'll touch my heart on the other side.

Canine Tip For pet loss counseling, contact Tufts University Pet Loss Support Hotline at (508) 839-7966 Monday through Friday, 6 to 9 P.M., or log on to www.tufts.edu/vet/petloss.

Pet Peeve #197
Ignoring Me on the Other Side

Once we are gone, don't tune us out if we try to contact you. Remember the movies *Ghost* and *City of Angels*? It irks me to think that there may be dog angels and their humans won't listen to their sounds. Don't count us totally out just because our dog bodies are gone. Our spirits will be with you forever.

Grr-eat Solution Keep an open mind. Often we come back in dreams to say our final good-byes. My human, for example, told me the story of Carmella, her yellow Lab. Soon after her dog passed, she had a dream that Carmella was on the beach frolicking and re-trieving her favorite Frisbee. If you see us in a dream, please see it as a special message. Don't delete it. It's like a special message from doggy heaven. Please respond.

Canine Tip To experience an after-life dog reunion, contact a pet psychic, who specializes in contacting deceased pets. Some pet psychics, such as Mary Getten, have websites (www.marygetten. com); others give telephone consultations.

Pet Peeve #198
Slave–Master Relationship

While our canine rights have expanded, it boggles my Bird Dog brain how some humans still treat their dogs like slaves. What gives? I am your best friend. So why would you ever want to do anything to jeopardize our canine–human bond? Dogs should set boundaries (actually I have), and when pushy people step over the line we must defend ourselves.

Grr-eat Solution Dr. Elliot Katz, president of In Defense of Animals, has a great philosophy, which I wish I had made up myself so it would be a Dylanology. Never mind, he says it best: "Our dream is to have every person, young and old, see and treat animals not as property to be exploited, abandoned, or killed, but as individuals who deserve consideration for their needs and quality of life. Our dream is fast becoming a reality as hundreds of thousands of caring people are throwing off the mantle of 'ownership' in favor of the caring mantle of 'guardianship.'"

So I've made a mini list of New Rules for humans and dogs. The following five rules are off the top of my head:

- Treat me as I would treat you.

- If you don't have anything nice to say, "no bark!"

- Tell me you love me every day.

- Talk to me with respect.

- Most important, remember that I have feelings just like you do.

Pet Peeve #199
Making Me Kiss Up

Yeah, we dogs provide unconditional doggy kisses, but we're not dumb, nor do we forget (well, at twelve and a half I do have my senior moments). When you have a bad day and take it out on the dog, it's unfair. Later on, you'll come to us all happy again and sniffing around for dog affection and expect us to be there like always. No attitude, no airs. Please. If a human gave you the hot-and-cold treatment would you always be forgiving? I don't think so.

Grr-eat Solution We dogs have emotions and we don't like to be toyed with. If you do something that leaves me thinking "bad human!" you need to make amends before you get my doggy kisses and I forgive you. Don't always expect us to be there for you wagging our tails and ready to play. Dogs, like humans, have feelings that get hurt. And in my case, as a sensitive senior Brittany, I wear my heart on my sleeve, and giving out doggy kisses to my human means something to me.

Pet Peeve #200
No Doggy Kisses

Why do some people act like our doggy smooches are disgusting? As long as we are kept on a regular doggy dental plan, our kisses should not be shunned by the ones we love. If humans duck when their beloved dog wants to give them a doggy kiss, I think it stinks. Those humans don't deserve our love and devotion.

Grr-eat Solution Doggy kisses are acceptable these days. I've seen kids, parents, and grandparents be kissed by their pooch. And often dog people will kiss us on our nose in return. It's a wonderful way to enhance the canine–human bond.

Pet Peeve #201
Treating Me Like I'm Human

While I want to be treated with human respect (this includes acceptance of my doggy kisses), I am still a dog. Some humans can't face this simple fact. For instance, explains Dr. Coren, if we do something wrong, one of the members of the family will come up and chastise us by barking, "How many times have I told you not to do that?" We just sit there with a blank stare because we don't understand a word that is being said. And finally, the person says, "Oh, you're just so stupid."

"People presume that we're going to respond in natural human arguments," points out Dr. Coren. Not so. We don't understand what you're talking about. We don't get that it is wrong to go into the waste can and drag tissues all over the place. Hello. We are a dog, not a human.

Grr-eat Solution "Ignore bad behavior and reward good behavior," says Dr. Coren. In other words, when we do something that upsets you, let it go because we don't get it. If we could get your message we would put our paws over our ears and chant "La-la-la-la-la." The bottom line: Reward us when we do good and mum is the word otherwise.

Pet Peeve #202
Telling Me to Act Like a Cat

Out of all of these 101 pet peeves, this one takes the cake. How do you expect a dog to take the human comment, "Why can't you act more like a cat?" If we are in your life and you can't accept us as we are, it can hurt our doggy feelings. Cats don't care about human acceptance as much as dogs do. They will just lick their paws and walk away. Remember, dogs are people-pleasers. No, I won't purr, meow, or stalk a bird (well, maybe I'll do that). Dogs do dog things. And it bugs us when humans want us to exhibit more catlike traits.

Grr-eat Solution Personally, I want my human to accept my canine personality. I run, bark, and chew bones. My point is, I am a dog. I am loyal (always) and obedient (usually). If you want dogs to act more like cats, perhaps you are in the wrong department. (Go back to Part One: "Your Feline's 101 Pet Peeves.") I am Dog. Hear me bark. Hug me and I will respond with a doggy kiss. ("Woof!")

© Paul Tsang

CAL OREY is an accomplished author and journalist. She has a master's degree in English (creative writing) from San Francisco State University and in the past decade has written hundreds of articles for a variety of national-al magazines. She specializes in topics as diverse as health, nutrition, relationships, and pets. Her articles on pets have appeared in publications such as *Woman's World, Complete Woman, Dog World, AKC Gazette,* and *Dog Fancy,* and on the Web sites www.PetPlace.com and www.allpets.com. Ms. Orey is also the author of *The Essential Guide to Natural Pet Care: Cancer, The Essential Guide to Natural Pet Care: Epilepsy,* and *Doctors' Orders: What 101 Doctors Do to Stay Healthy.* She lives in Northern California.

DYLAN is a pedigreed Brittany who is registered with the American Kennel Club. He has been Cal Orey's muse in several pet publications and in books such as *The Essential Guide to Natural Pet Care: Epilepsy.* He is a fun-loving, energetic senior dog who loves to run, swim, point, and chase imaginary birds. Born on September 22, he is a sensitive and intellectual Virgo on the cusp of Libra, which gives him canine charisma and a people-loving nature.

KEROUAC, aka K.C., is a mixed-breed domestic longhaired cat who was saved by a private rescue organization in the California Sierras. He was able to sit still long enough to get a master's degree in Meow Meow from San Francisco State University. He wrote *On the Fence,* his best-known and most popular book, in just three weeks, typing on empty cat litter bags. He is a chatty Gemini and a self-assured cat with a mind of his own. He was the author of the www.allpets.com "Dear Kerouac" column.